Mortimer Collins

A fight with fortune

Vol. 2

Mortimer Collins

A fight with fortune
Vol. 2

ISBN/EAN: 9783337132323

Printed in Europe, USA, Canada, Australia, Japan

Cover: Foto ©Andreas Hilbeck / pixelio.de

More available books at **www.hansebooks.com**

A FIGHT WITH FORTUNE.

BY

MORTIMER COLLINS.

IN THREE VOLUMES.

VOL. II.

LONDON:
HURST AND BLACKETT, PUBLISHERS,
13, GREAT MARLBOROUGH STREET.
1876.

A FIGHT WITH FORTUNE.

CHAPTER I.

LONDON.

Astrologos.—If London be the world's most noble city, then
 Who dwells therein should be no common citizen,
 The world's most noble title, greater far than all
 Dukes, but not *duces*, Earls not free from churlishness,
 Should be the sounding civic name of Londoner.
Rafael.—Lofty ideal! But the race of cockneys are
 As commonplace a set as you'll see anywhere ;
 A race that loves the billiard-room and music-hall,
 And tripe and onions, and hot spirits afterward.
Astrologos.—Wait, Count, until you meet a perfect Londoner,
 A man who knows that City's penetralia,
 Master of fashion, politics, and gaiety,
 Swimmer on summit wave of choice society.
 A Londoner, my lord, is not *fæx Londini ;*

He lives in Clubland, gossips at the Travellers',
Checkmates a Bishop at the Athenæum ; and
Loiters away to play whist at the Arlington.
Dining alone, his dinner is a work of art ;
And, dining out, his wit turns meal to festival.
Always himself, cool, easy, careless, nonchalant,
Whether he helps a fair Princess to strawberries
(Bright eyes may languish under Royal eyelashes)
Or heads a merry crew to Richmond, wondering
Which they like best, the Heidseck or the nightingales.
ALOUETTE.—Papa, I should so like to know a Londoner.

The Comedy of Dreams.

A LL roads lead to Rome. It might
have been true once, that saying ;
but now-a-days all roads lead to London.
Aspiring poet, with epic or drama ; youthful politician, with a tongue to sell and a
party to choose ; peer of the realm, embarrassed by too much money ; swindler,
with a diamond mine in the Herzegovina ;
pretty heiress, who can be content with
nothing less than a Duke ; young woman

from the country, who thinks the kitchen of a lodging-house more charming than the meadows where she has been wont to milk deep-uddered kine—all these go to London.

" Non cuivis homini contingit adire Corinthum,"

says Horace. True, no doubt; but your modern Londoner altogether outdoes the Corinthian. For wisdom and folly, pleasure and anguish, goodness and wickedness, beauty and hideousness, force and feeble-ness—-for all the contrasts of humanity— London is unrivalled. And to be a true Londoner is to know the highest sublimity and the deepest abasement possible to mankind. Your cool citizen of the world's chief city, amazed at nothing, amused by everything, analyses and appraises a speech by Disraeli or Kenealy, a poem by Browning or Gibbs, even as the citizens of Athens judged Aristophanes and Alcibiades. Your true Londoner is a man of infinite possibilities, who carefully avoids performance. He is a man who *could* do anything he pleased to absolute perfection; but he does not choose to do anything. His mission is to criticise those who do imperfectly what he could do perfectly, were it only worth his while. It is not. London is to him a theatre; he takes a perpetual stall, and calmly watches the gradual development of the marvellous drama of life, in which every scene is a surprise, in which nothing is certain but the unforeseen.

The City crucible condenses intellect; and the man who knows his London knows a good deal of humanity. It is a curiously special art. Captain Webb could never have swum the Channel if his bones were not light, if his tendency were not somewhat adipose. This I say with certainty, never having seen him or heard anything of his physique. Similarly, a man cannot be a thorough Londoner unless his brain is light enough to float nautilus-like on the surface of the social tide, unless his resistant power is strong enough to defy the scandal of dowagers and the epigrams of rivals. No Englishman is educated who has not known London. It is the only absolute university. We all graduate there, from statesman to burglar, from poet to penny-a-liner. But London should be strictly regarded as a University. No man should remain in it regularly after the time when his intellect comes of age,

which is somewhere about forty. When
that terrible eighth lustrum arrives (terrible only to the precocious, who are
hardened cynics at five and twenty), try
life in the country. See London at intervals. Don't let the swift world slip by and
leave you far behind the ideas of the time.
They may not be brilliant or original ideas,
but it is just as well to know them. The
recitatives of Tyndall and Huxley and
Darwin are not to me as the songs of
Homer and Shakespeare; "the words of
Mercury are harsh after the songs of
Apollo;" but let us learn what these prosy
gentry have to say, lest by any means we
should miss some great saying of a nobler
kind. London cannot be an insignificant
city while Robert Browning and Thomas
Carlyle are among its inhabitants; but,

alas! how long is it since either poet or philosopher gave us a new thought, or even the old thought newly put? London, to say once more what I said at first, is the University of the world; it attracts the rarest loveliness and the vilest ugliness, the ablest rogue and the most absolute fool.

It amuses and instructs to compare London with Paris. Was it Coleridge who said that France is a monarchy, with a Republic for its capital? Paris does not represent France in the least degree, whereas London is merely intensified England. The country squire has his park: so has the Londoner, and they are Royal parks—therefore the heritage of the people. As every country gentleman may, some day or other, be Lord Lieutenant, or at least

High Sheriff, so every civic Londoner may
become Lord Mayor, every West End
Londoner the leader of fashion, a far
higher dignity. The country squire ex-
amines with great care his hot-houses,
pineries, melon-pits, vineries, carp ponds :
it is a daily pleasure to him. The Londoner
finds the fairest of all fruit in Covent Garden, and the freshest of all fish in Billingsgate. Nor is this all. If you love good
pictures, rare old books, quaint and sug-
gestive, fine wine, enticing comestibles, try
to learn London. There is one street in
which you shall find delicious song birds;
and another in which carved oak furniture
abounds; and another in which you may
pick up an *editio princeps ;* and another in
which glass is elegant and cheaply to be
bought. I might run through an inter-

minable catalogue. London is simply the Microcosm, and to an uncultured stranger fresh from the country London was not easily intelligible. Charles Cotton had not only intelligence, but that far higher faculty—imagination. To understand London when you first see it, the work of a well-trained intelligence, is no trivial matter; but to comprehend it before seeing it, and even if you never see it, tests the great imaginative faculty—the king of the brain. It can be done : else how could Homer tell us all we need to know of Troy, which he never saw till the mighty son of Peleus had long passed to the fields of asphodel ? Troy had its Piccadilly and its Park Lane. London hath its Hector and its Paris. Even Cressida——but at this delicate point I pause.

Charles Cotton, a mere villager, was much perplexed by his first vision of London. But he soon grew in mental culture to understand it. Fools do not grow in mental culture. A dull fellow, who has been carefully educated, will break down under a new situation. It is not so with a man, however uneducated, who possesses imaginative vitality. To Charles Cotton, London was a home. He saw that he could always live in a city with such infinite requirements. Gay and joyous in the consciousness of perfect health and easy capacity for work, he made up his mind that London was an oyster easy to open, and with a pearl a safe find therein. He laughed at difficulty. He plunged into the perilous London ocean, an unaccustomed swimmer, with the certainty that the time would come for him to feel at home in those troublous waters. He took his header into London life as readily as into the London river when he saved a poor young girl from drowning.

She was a tall fair woman of nearly thirty, with abundant yellow hair of that colour which it is the foolish fashion to imitate by dyeing. She was got on board the steamer, and speedily resuscitated, for hers was a strong constitution, and the daring plunge had done her little harm. Then came the questions, Who was she? What to do with her? Legally, she ought to have been given into custody for an attempt to commit suicide, but the captain of the steamer was a kind-hearted fellow, and desired to evade the law on that point. The young woman, when brought to her-

self, was sulky; nothing would she say
about herself, and the skipper began to
get tired of her obstinacy. Cotton, who
had been arrayed in a spare suit of the
worthy commander's clothes, much too
small for him everywhere except the waist,
suggested that Monsieur Dulau should for
the present take charge of her. He had
a kind of intuition that he should not have
fished this woman out of the Thames unless
she was intended to be of some use to him.
There was not much time for discussion on
board a river steamer; wherefore, as Cotton
was impulsive, and Dulau passive, and the
captain in a devil of a hurry, it resulted in
the fair-haired suicide being landed at
Westminster in the best costume that
could be arranged for her. She did
not look elegant, though naturally what

would be styled a fine woman. Nobody looks particularly charming in another fellow's clothes. This is true of the male sex, as I have proved, having, wet through up in the Lakes, been glad to wear the togs of a jolly Westmerland landlord, about five feet high, and almost the same in breadth. I was a boy of nineteen, six feet in my socks, and thin as a lath. Guy as I was, and much as the lasses laughed to see me, I enjoyed my broiled mutton ham and claret, and my bed of fresh heather, and was quite ready for char at breakfast. But nobody can quite carry off unfitting apparel, and this poor girl, clad in some raiment which belonged to the captain's wife, accidentally left on board, looked perfectly unhappy. She probably wished her attempt at suicide had been a success.

Dulau and Cotton hurried her into a cab and drove home. Dulau was not happy in his mind about it. He wondered what would his wife say or think. Had he not regarded Cotton as a *protégé* of the Marquis, he would not have allowed him to bring the woman to his highly respectable establishment. What would Madame say? This was what perplexed Dulau, who had a proper respect for the chief of the household.

To his delight, Madame took the affair kindly. She liked the look of Charles Cotton, a handsome young Englishman, with plenty of pluck; and she was fond of a romance. So she took the young woman, fresh from Thames, in hand, and tried to get something out of her, but she

might as well have tried to get blood out
of a diamond or Roederer from a Good
Templar. She continued sullen, though
professing a great amount of gratitude to
the man who had saved her life, but she
would not say who she was or where she
lived. Madame Dulau was naturally disgusted.

" I won't have that *misérable* here,
Achille," she said. " Let her go. Why
Monsieur Cotton did not allow her to
drown I cannot understand. It would have
been the best thing for her."

But Dulau induced his wife to let the
poor creature stay, and it was fortunate
that he did so. She was put into a room
upstairs, and made comfortable. It was
Cotton's wish, and Cotton's natural im-
petuosity was backed by the paramount

influence of Castelcicala, so there was the tall yellow-haired suicidal failure sulking in an attic, when the Marquis de Castelcicala turned up at Dulau's in the evening. There was a pleasantly inaccurate account of the attempt at suicide, printed on pink paper, by an evening journal; but the Marquis had not seen this, as he hated pink paper. Indeed, he had a general detestation of newspapers, resting on the theory (wholly incorrect of course) that their news is often false, and that their opinions based on that news are always wrong. I confess that I am sorry for Castelcicala, who could not appreciate the wisdom and experience which are found in the English newspaper editor. We go in for potted omniscience in this great country; if the inferior European States cannot perceive our success in this direction, we can only be sorry for them. Some people would say, pray for them ; but I do not go so far as that.

CHAPTER II.

THE PEER'S CAPRICE.

ASTROLOGOS.—Ambition has, my lord, unknown develop-
　　　　ments,
　　　And when a man has squeezed the sponge of
　　　　life enough
　　　To satisfy the multitude, he yearns once more
　　　For something utterly beyond the multitude,
　　　Something immeasurable, mad, impossible.
RAPHAEL.—With such a man, I have the strongest sym-
　　　　pathy :
　　　My sorrow is, to me there's nought impossible.
ALOUTTE (aside).—Make love to me, fair prince, and see
　　　　what comes of it.
　　　　　　　　　　　　　　The Comedy of Dreams.

WHY in the world should Bellasys
want fifty thousand pounds? Where
in the world was Crake to get that sum in

a day? Let us deal with the second question first. Look at the advertisements of the leading London papers, and you will see announced various co-operative schemes which are supposed to open a royal road to fortune. One society, if you deal with its associated tradesmen, kindly guarantees that all the money you spend on meat and drink and clothing shall in due time be returned to you; whence it is clear that there is no longer any truth in the old proverb, *Ex nihilo nihil fit.* Another whose fluent lecturer seems to have made a slight impression on the Town of Steel, proposes a confederation of working men to surpass the superb financial achievements of the Barings and the Rothschilds. The idea has a grandeur almost oppressive. If a million working men were to subscribe a sovereign each, and put it in the hands of a financier who was honest, and could wisely manipulate a million sterling, it would in due time be decupled; but when this ideal financier had got his ten millions, might it not be too much for his honesty? There are a good many things a sovereign will buy: trowsers, shoes, dinners, wine, lie within the limit of that convenient yellow disc.

Now Crake, a wise man in his generation, had originated a co-operative scheme long before these fumblers tried to do something in that way. Crake was by profession a thief, and was proud thereat. He found out, with those ferret eyes of his, a few other gentlemen who were thieves, but who could not steal scientifically. They were dumb poets, so to speak.

Crake took then in hand, and used them wisely. Their joint capital was so utilised as to produce much more than that ideal eighteen per cent. which is the offer made by modern co-operation.

Crake, in promising Lord Bellasys fifty thousand pounds by two o'clock next day, had made a heavy pull on his resources. He had not above twenty thousand pounds in the Bank of England at the moment, and there were small amounts, a thousand or two, to come out of that. So he was in the City at an early hour the next morning, to meet his syndicate. The place of meeting was a dingy hole in Little Saint Thomas Apostle. Three of his comrades met him; he explained the business briefly, and they were quite ready.

" Bellasys is safe," said one man. " Can't

think why he wants it, for I never knew him borrow money before."

"Perhaps he wants a new sensation," said another. "If so, I think borrowing money as likely to amuse him as anything."

The third, who was a very pious gentleman, and a great benefactor to the suburban church at which he worshipped, said nothing; but it was arranged that Crake should have the money at once, and he drove off with it, a tempting bundle of crisp notes, to Long's Hotel, reaching that well-known pleasant hostelry at a few minutes before twelve. He was not the sort of fellow that the hotel in question welcomes gleefully; and the waiter, when he asked for Lord Bellasys, looked at him with a slightly scrutinising eye. But

Frederick, the waiter aforesaid, was aware that Lord Bellasys was a man without need to fear attorneys, sheriffs' officers, and the whole vile crew who live upon the recklessness of gentlemen which they assiduously encourage. So Crake found his way, at a little past noon, to his lordship's sitting-room.

No one there, of course. Preparations for breakfast, in the form of a lobster, a perigord pie, sundry tall bottles of various wines. No Lord Bellasys. "Little he cares for fifty thou'," thought Crake. Presently the door opened, and in came the Honourable Clarence Vere, fresh as paint, with a gardenia in his buttonhole.

"Ha, Crake," said he, "here you are! Nothing like business. Don't forget the cheque for commission, you old villain."

"His lordship doesn't seem in a hurry for the money," said Crake.

"Bellasys in a hurry for anything! When you see that announce the day of judgment. You're a cool hand, Crake, but you're not so cool as Bellasys."

Presently Bellasys entered, looking fresh and bright, with a twinkle of fun in his eye. He liked a lark. There was no harm in this man, but he looked on the sunny side of life.

"Just in time for breakfast, old Crake," he said. "Ring the bell, Clarry. They promised me something special this morning, because I came home early last night. Got in by two, by Jove! I think the most difficult thing in these days is getting to bed."

Breakfast was served in Jubber's finest

style. Crake scarcely knew himself. Nothing was wanting that Billingsgate or Leadenhall or Covent Garden could supply. The wine, which comes straight from the grower, was perfect. The old thief and usurer and scamp of all work almost melted into humanity as he ate and drank. Bellasys, who was what few people imagined him—an observer of human nature,—was greatly amused by Crake.

The entertainment ended with caviare on toast, and a Sillery *sec* which would have made Thackeray happy. It was nearly two o'clock. Vere, who had been for some time wondering when business was to begin, said suddenly,

" Are you going down to Fulham this morning, Bellasys ? It groweth late."

Bellasys looked at his watch.

"True, my friend. I must move. Have you got that small sum of money, Crake? Here's my cheque."

He took it from his waistcoat-pocket, and carelessly threw it to the usurer, who on his part at once handed over Bank of England notes to the amount of £50,000. Bellasys shoved them carelessly into the side pocket of his morning coat; then, rising, he said,

"Thanks, Crake. Good morning. You'll find the cheque all right." And he walked out of the room.

Now comes the other question, placed first, to be answered second. Why in the world should Lord Bellasys want to borrow £50,000 at 60 per cent.? Why could not this owner of vast estates take things easily, and use his property wisely? Well, as a fact, fifty thousand was rather more than he could call up on the instant, for he was lucky in having a sagacious steward, who did not starve the estates. A queer mixture of common sense and madness was Bellasys. He encouraged his steward in careful management, and never demanded from him an unusual money supply; but he indulged many wild whims, which he could easily do out of his vast income. However, he had just now thought on the wildest whim of all, and it was to gratify it he went to Crake for this £50,000. It was a trifle to a man with a third of a million a year.

Now to reveal the whim. Bellasys had seen Lady Elfrida Fontenoy, daughter of a Duke and full of unsatisfied ambitions, and had taken a slight fancy to her, which she had returned fifty-fold. In fact he found that it was almost necessary for him to run away with her : and, although he was a good deal puzzled what he should do with her thereafter, in his wild mood he thought he would risk it. He had a great contempt for her father, the Duke of Derwentwater, the richest and prosiest of the ducal hierarchy. So he let Lady Elfrida have her wilful way, met her and her maid, very much muffled up, at Water-loo Station, and took them off to Southampton, where his yacht was waiting for him.

It was a dull enough journey. Lady Elfrida was already in a repentant state. Bellasys, who would have been gay enough if really interested in the lady with whom he was eloping, was longing all the way for a cigar. Never had the line from London to Southampton seemed so desperately dreary. The maid was luckiest of the two : she slept.

La femme propose. When the great seaport was reached at last, the first person Bellasys saw on the platform was Lord Robert Fontenoy, Elfrida's brother. That young gentleman was noted for coolness. He came up to Bellasys in a quiet way and said,

" Ah, old fellow, glad to see you have taken care of Elfrida. I will relieve you of your charge. She is going to Fontenoy with me. Glad to see you there, at any time."

Bellasys was relieved. He took his hat off to the lady, and drove to Radley's Hotel, heartily thankful for the invention of the telegraph.

CHAPTER III.

DAPHNE AND APOLLO.

APOLLO.—I Claros-isle and Tenedos command.
DAPHNE.—Thank ye, I would not leave my native land.
PRIOR.

WHEN the Marquis reached Dulau's and heard what had occurred, he was much amused.

"Who is the woman?" he asked.

"No one knows," said Dulau, "and she will not tell."

"So you saved her life without knowing

anything about her," said Castelcicala.
" Was the game worth the candle? And
why bring her here? Surely you might
have let her find her way home."

" It is my fault," said Cotton. " I had
a superstitious feeling that I had saved
her life for some purpose. It was stupid,
I fear."

" Of course it was," laughed the Marquis.
" All human actions are stupid. Yet,
somehow, our very stupidity is sometimes
better than wisdom. Success is often due
to wholesale blundering. Waterloo was
won by mistake, according to the best
military authorities. Let us leave this
young person till morning, when possibly
I may get something out of her. How do
you like London, Cotton?"

" I already feel at home in it," he said.

" It seems to me a city in which any man, able and willing to work, may live and may enjoy life. I am eager to see more of it."

" So you shall. We will see a little of London together this evening. Let us go and dine."

Cotton's notion of dinner was middiurnal, but he knew that patricians dined when plebeians supped, and he accepted the Marquis's offer with laudable coolness. Sending for a hansom, Castelcicala took the young villager farther west. It amused him to see the villager turn Londoner so quickly. " That's the strong point with these English," he thought; " nothing astonishes them. If you took an English minnow out of a brook, and threw him into the Atlantic, he'd become a whale, or at least a sword-fish."

Lycett's. Do you know it, courteous reader? The Marquis and Cotton passed through a long corridor, with cool lavatories, and entered a lofty room with wide windows looking on a patrician thoroughfare. Tall mirrors, paintings on the panel of game and fruit, vaulted ceiling with the Rape of Proserpine by Thornhill or one of his disciples, stern old Pluto flogging four horses abreast with one hand, while the other encircled the lady's nude waist, made a curious impression on the young man's mind. The waiters were all dressed in a green livery, with knee breeches and buckled shoes—and powdered hair.

"Tell Lycett I wish to see him," said the Marquis to one of these tall fellows, taking his seat where a table was invitingly niched in a bow window. "Sit down, Cotton. You get here the best dinner in the world."

"I have found a steak and a pint of beer the best dinner in the world before now," said the glazier.

"Appetite makes dinner, as imagination makes poetry. Ah, here comes Lycett."

There appeared a short lively gentleman of seventy, with white hair, in irreproach- able evening dress, with diamond studs in his snowy linen shirt. He bowed to the Marquis with marvellous elegance.

"I have not seen you for a long while," said Castelcicala. "Now I want a nice little dinner for my friend, who has brought a grand unsophisticated appetite to Lon- don. What shall we give him?"

Lycett put up his gold-rimmed glasses,

and eyed Cotton curiously. A young fellow with an appetite! His business was to create appetite by excellence of viand. He thought a rumpsteak was the best thing for a fellow like Cotton. Still the Marquis must have his way. So the oracle spoke.

" Half-a-dozen oysters, and Montrachet; clear turtle and punch; red mullet stewed in port; Champagne; fillet of beef; Chambertin; grouse, with Yquem; gruyère; nectarines and figs; Chartreuse and Noyau."

Lycett rattled off his whimsical bill of fare in the rapid style of Charles Mathews and Albert Smith—the Marquis accepted it with amusement, and in less than a quarter of an hour the oysters were there, and the other courses followed with perfect regularity. Charles Cotton took the whole matter coolly, though never before in his life had he tasted mullet or turtle or grouse, Montrachet or Chartreuse. He held the theory that what a man eats and drinks, is less important than what a man does and thinks. His perfectly simple comments on the whole entertainment greatly amused the Marquis. He smiled to see that he preferred Noyau to Chartreuse, and nectarines to figs. Really the palate demands as much education as the brain.

" Shall we go to a theatre ?" said the Marquis presently. " We shall be in time for the ballet at the Caprice, where I have a box."

" I have never been at a theatre, except at a country fair," said Cotton. "But I have read Shakespeare."

"His caprices, superb as they were, will not prepare you for the Caprice. Come and see for yourself."

They drove to this pleasant little theatre. The Marquis had a stage box on a lower level than the stage itself. The ballet was mythological—turning on that story well known to all readers of Lempriere's Dictionary and Mangnall's Questions, the pursuit of Daphne by Apollo. Apollo was played by a superb female of about five feet ten, whereas Daphne was a little creature not above five feet, and as lively as a bird; and these were the principal actors all through. Burlesque words were wedded to charming music; and Apollo wooed Daphne and Daphne defied Apollo in dances which rather astonished Charles Cotton's weak mind.

"As a study of legs," said the Marquis, using his opera glass, "I consider this scene perfect."

Apollo was dashing after Daphne. She, pirouetting around the stage, with attitudes that might make a virtuous Lord Chamberlain blush, laughed at his attempts. Suddenly he came to the front of the stage, and she, lightly leaping on his shoulder, sang—

> "Poor dear Apollo!
> Couldn't he follow?
> Does he get older, the god of the sun?
> Nymphs were afraid of him:
> Now they have made of him
> Just a mere joke, for his courage is done.
>
> "Poor dear Apollo!
> The girls beat him hollow,
> Soon he will sadly be tearing his hair:
> Where are his laurels
> And manners and morals?
> Echo replies that she doesn't know where."

Daphne sang. Apollo caught her by the ancle. She, freeing herself from his grip, turned rather an indecorous somersault, designed to display her form. Display of form, when natural, is the true thing; when theatrical, and done with a purpose, it is nasty. This feeling fell upon Charles Cotton, a sensible young fellow, with the idea in his head that a woman is too beautiful to be in the least degree sullied by immodesty. He had fallen in love with an ideal girl, a creature who might some day stand

"... like some Greek Lady of the Skies,
In marble carved for millions to admire,"

and for him only to love and to have. And, having thus fallen in love, he could not endure the thought of any woman lowering herself to the mere exhibition of her form for money. Apollo and Daphne gave him a sick feeling. His face showed his disgust, for the Marquis said,

" You don't like this ?"

" No, indeed."

" Nor I. When, in the old Greek processions, boys and girls walked naked, there was no harm, because there was no design of harm. But this sort of thing is abominable, and I shall give up my box at the Caprice."

"1 know nothing of theatres," said Charles Cotton, as they walked homewards, being unable to get a cab, " but I cannot help thinking they do more harm than good, if what I have seen to-night is a fair specimen."

" Fair !" quoth the Marquis, " I can show you stranger things. But I will wait till you have learnt a little more of this wild stern London."

" Do people really enjoy the kind of dancing I have just seen ?" asked Cotton.

" It goes on night after night, for hundreds of nights together."

" How strange ! I should have thought it would have disgusted everybody. I never want to see anything of the sort again."

" Once is enough," said Castelcicala to himself. " That boy's ideas are pure. I like him. I hope England has plenty of the same stamp."

They went home together, and the Marquis had his customary room, always kept for him by Dulau. Next morning he obtained permission to visit the lady whom Cotton had saved from what is commonly known as a watery grave. She was still in a sulky state, and possibly might have made another plunge from the bridge had she been anywhere near it. She was red-eyed, hectic, excited.

"Just tell me," said the Marquis, with commanding coolness, "why you threw yourself into the river."

The girl shrank back into a corner of the room, holding her long yellow hair with both hands; but his strong keen glance followed and fixed her.

"Tell me," he said again, in accents of unmistakeable resolve.

"I wanted to get away from horrid slavery," she said, sobbing terribly. "I am so tired of that dreadful man! I married him down at Kent, ten years ago, when I was just come into a little money,

and I was a fool, and he was handsome
and boastful. O good God! how could I
know he was a coward and a thief? And
now I am tied to him all my life. O, I
wish that young man had left me alone
and let me drown!"

"Don't be foolish," said the Marquis,
with a caressing kindness which he always
used to women in distress. "You have
had terrible misfortunes, but you should
not try to escape from them in a wicked
way. For a good woman to be married to
a bad man is dreadful, but she ought still
to try to be good. Is this man doing
anything very wicked just now?"

"O, I don't know, sir," she sobbed. "I
think I heard him say to a pal he was
going after diamonds. They call him the
Parson. O dear, dear, dear me! how

well I remember when I saw him first, on
Tunbridge Cricket Ground! I thought what
a handsome man he was. And to think
what has come of it, and all my poor little
bit of money gone!"

Castelcicala was sadly impressed by
this poor woman, who was evidently fit
for a better career. He saw, however,
that, by her accidental appearance on the
scene, there was a better chance of re-
gaining the Squire's diamonds. The moment she told him her story he sprang to
the conclusion; and he decided that by
means of this woman, accidentally rescued
by Cotton, the diamonds might be traced.
A difficult and delicate task, seeing that
a woman who knows her husband to be a
thief, and feels him to be a brute, will try
to save him from harm. What can be

said ?   Women are women.   There is nobody who can understand them, and nobody who can help loving them.

CHAPTER IV.

FALCONRY.

"'The hawk soars high. A flutter in the heronry."

YES. When the falcon soars, the heron flutters. The Marquis returned from London to Englehurst, with a thin thread of discovery running through his brain, which he had left in the hands of the detectives. He had also left Charles Cotton at M. Dulau's establishment, with perfect instructions as to what he had better do. The Marquis had his reasons for a rapid return. The diamonds would be rescued, he felt pretty sure; but he was thinking of a pearl of girls—Cis Englehurst.

Castelcicala was a philosopher as well as a poet, and he thought over this question very carefully. He was Italian; she English; he was a dozen or fifteen years her elder. Was it possible she could care for him? Castelcicala was not agonizingly in love; if a woman refused him he would simply think she was rather a fool for doing so. And he would have some justification, since he was a man who would worship the lady he loved in poetic fashion. He was true knight and troubadour. To him a lady was a divinity. Such men are rather rare in these days of the Divorce Court and the breach of promise action ; but they still exist. To put it tersely, there are a few gentlemen who believe in the existence of ladies. That such should be the case is a remarkable fact. The loud woman, the fast woman, the scientific woman, have done their utmost to abolish the lady. Ah, but without success. She lives still, in happy corners of England where progress is unknown, and where she grows, a joyous radiant flower, unspoiled by algebraic or ecclesiastic watering-pot. There are plenty of lovely girls in England who know absolutely nothing—those are the sweet creatures from whom to choose wives. The instant they begin to talk about the Athanasian Creed or the Darwinian theory they are useless for marriagable purposes.

Castelcicala came back, told the Squire

things were in train, and the diamonds would probably be restored, and then tempted Cecilia to try her falcons. He wanted to fill her gay young head with joyous romance, all connected with him. On the river Engle there was a grand heronry, and the glorious birds were to be seen fishing the stream at all hours of the day; but chiefly at eventide, when the sunset fell upon the shallows, the herons if startled flew away into the sunset as if they were a part of it. Many a time had Cis Englehurst watched them in her somewhat solitary girlhood, rising suddenly into the purple sky with magic mockery of its divine colours. It had been a delight to her to sit on the banks of the Engle, with her favourite poet to dream over, and to see the calm tall birds fishing

the pools, and then to watch them soaring
away into the glory of the west.

Now who was Cis Englehurst's favourite
poet? Should you care much, O investi-
gative reader, for a girl whose ideal was
Rosetti or Swinburne or Tennyson? I
shouldn't. If you meet with a girl who
understands her Shakespeare, you find a
lady of Rosalind's delicious type. Whereas,
when you encounter an adorer of Tupper
. . . no, I can't finish that sentence. Our
pretty Cis did not roam in the wide regions
which Shakespeare has filled with life and
love, with grandeur and glory; but she
did not read Tupper. No: Cis's pet poet
was Keats: and how many delicious
dreams she dreamt over *The Eve of St.
Agnes,* over those divine odes inspired by
a nightingale and a Greek urn, and quite

without parallel in our literature! There are much greater things, but these are unique—the work of an unclassical Englishman who was Greek by intuition. Sophocles, the nightingale of Colonos, would have envied them.

So Cis read Keats by the Engle, and watched the herons. And her study of that poet led her to in some measure understand Castelcicala's romantic character. For the Marquis looked on life with that calm delight which is noticeable in the later poems of Keats; he loved the beauty of the world and the beauty of women; he enjoyed existence with a kind of industrious indolence. The fierce passion felt or affected by certain modern writers was wholly out of his line : he was cavalier and troubadour, and could love a lady and de-

fend her against the world, but he could
not writhe and sweat and . . . make a
brute of himself. . His brain was as clear
as his rapier, and his laugh as true as his
oath. He looked on life as to be lived
wisely, and thereby happily. He looked
on Cis Englehurst as the most lovely creature with unawakened heart that he had
seen, and he felt a joyous ambition to win
her. But, if he failed, if another man
won, why he would wish them both the
highest happiness, and would do all he
could to secure it. Such was the Castelcicala's temper. He had no idea of an only
possible she. Perhaps he was rather too
great an admirer of all lovely ladies to
throw his whole soul into an absolute in-
satiable passion for one.

However, he worshipped Cis Englehurst,

who dreamt the hours away without thought of love. She wandered in Keats's calm forest-ground, where there is no revelation of human passion, but only a mingling of mystery and myth. She was very happy; a spoilt child with the kindest of fathers; no trouble in the past save her mother's loss; no fear in the future; nothing but a happy present to enjoy in all its heights and depths. O, to drink the divine wine of life from so clear a chalice! But, as the Epicurean poet says,

> ". . . medio de fonte leporum
> Surgit amari aliquid."

Pretty soft-eyed dreamy Cis, that "amari aliquid" will somehow reach you. Man, which includes girl, is born to trouble, as the sparks fly upwards.

The first day of hawking was very

pleasant. There was the Squire on his dark brown weight-carrier, a horse that seemed built for his master. Cis was on a gentle chestnut mare, and, with a tercel gentle on her gloved wrist, looked altogether ready for sport. Castelcicala rode a rather fidgety bay that he had taken in hand because the grooms were afraid of it, and were spoiling it. Rough usage made it savage ; it merely wanted a light hand and a good temper. The Marquis had hooded goshawk on wrist, and some of the people went down to Engle brink to scare a heron.

Up one soars, a purple and grey wonder in the sky. Castelcicala's falcon is unhooded, sees the soaring bird, flies like a shaft of lightning upward. The excitement is intense. Cis, though she loves the daring hawk, cannot help wishing the heron to escape; and there are tears in her bright eyes as the falcon, with pride of power, gets far above the heron, and prepares to swoop on its quarry. The hapless bird turns on its back in the air, and tries to defend itself with the claws that have put to death many an unlucky fish. Vain! The hawk falls on it like a thunderbolt; his fatal talons are in its brain; they descend together, a fluttering heap of feathers.

" O, how dreadful !" cried Cis.

Meanwhile the falconer had picked up the heron, and given the goshawk a lump of raw meat as a reward for his achievement.

There was more hawking that afternoon, and in time Cis Englehurst began to enjoy it. She pitied the beautiful herons at first, but the swift splendour and wild wonder of the hawks converted her to cruelty. I forget who remarked that women are by nature cruel, but there is just a little bit of truth in it. At the same time, I think that the woman who has gratified her taste for cruelty is always very sorry for it just after.

Cis Englehurst enjoyed her first gay afternoon of falconry, but it was not destined to end without an adventure. At a point above the Engle, where the wooded bank sloped about a hundred feet sheer down, Castelcicala was waiting for another heron to rise. He held his fidgety horse rather carelessly, and it suddenly started. A miserable boy with a penny whistle came across the heath; the Marquis's horse had never heard any noise so atrocious before, and did its utmost to get out of the way of it. Down the precipitous woodland rushed the horse; Castelcicala, taken by surprise, could only hold on by the thighs, and give him his head. He came down on his knees at the bottom of the descent, and his rider fell over his head, insensible.

Cis was there in two minutes. Her father rode round, but she, with quiet resolve, made her mare walk down the steep incline. By the time the Squire and his servants got round, Castelcicala was reviving. It was rather a pretty scene. There he lay, his curly head in her lap, while she bathed his brow with water from the Engle, and applied smelling-salts to his nostrils.

"This is what he wants, Cis," said the Squire, when he rode up. And he made the sufferer drink something from a flask, but what it was I venture not to say. It aroused the Marquis.

"I'm afraid that horse is done for, Englehurst," he said, raising himself rather reluctantly from his pleasant pillow. "It was my fault. He is easy enough when one has him well in hand. But I had got careless."

"And that brute of a boy came with his whistle," said the Squire. "I've told one of my fellows to thrash him well. Never mind the horse, my dear friend. Are you hurt much?"

"Any hurt would have been cured by the gentle relief I so soon received," said the Marquis. "It is quite worth while to be thrown from a horse to be so kindly treated afterwards."

" Cis went straight down after you, Marquis," said the Squire. " I galloped round."

Castelcicala looked up at the sharp descent. It seemed a hard matter for himself, a man who had risked his neck in a myriad ways. For Cecilia it was terrible. He was greatly moved. He wondered whether she loved him. But he only said, taking both her hands in his :—

" How brave and good you are !"

It is no new thing to say that you are apt to love those to whom you have done good. Nor, indeed, is it new that those who receive good too often hate the giver. I suppose this strange sad frailty of humanity is at the bottom of curious superstitions that work in uneducated minds; as, for instance, that if you save a person from drowning he will at some future time do you harm. It was my hap, in schoolboy days at Southsea, twice to save the same youngster from death; once, sleep-walking, he was on the point of throwing himself out of a window; the other time, trying to swim by the aid of bladders, he got his head under water and his feet in the air. In each case I chanced to be close enough to rescue him; and, as he never played me any rascally trick, as indeed I have never since heard of him, I think the old superstition may be disregarded.

Castelcicala had received a sharp shock. He looked somewhat pale and weak at dinner that day. Moreover, he was slightly angry with himself for having, after bringing the horse into order, forgotten for a moment the need of keeping its restless spirit under continuous control. It provoked this *preux chevalier* to have made even a momentary mistake. His was the haughty fiery spirit we find in the early ballads of Victor Hugo, written while he was still a poet:

> " Mon page, emplis mon escarcelle ;
> Velle
> Mon cheval de Calatrava :
> Va !"

In these days of £ s. d. there are yet a few men who decline to worship the £ s.-deity; and if, while so declining, they may perchance show a disproportionate delight in horse, hawk, hound, in woman, wine, wit, their critics have better reason to envy than to defame them.

CHAPTER V.

HUMAN FLOWERS.

Ore floridulo nitens,
Alba parthenice velut,
Luteumve papaver.

CATULLUS.

L OVELY Cis Englehurst pitied the
Marquis very much indeed. The
weary look of a man who has suffered a
severe shock gave paleness to his cheek;
but his eyes were as bright as ever, perchance a trifle brighter, since they were
lighted by the thought of her courageous

kindness in forcing her way straight to where he lay insensible. He wondered whether she loved him a little. Perhaps after all the gallant girl would have done the same for any man. Well, one thing was certain; not one woman in five thousand would have ridden down that perilous slope to help a man in trouble.

That evening Castelcicala went early to his rooms, much needing rest. Just before he went Cecilia had sung a quaint little canzonet, made and married to music by some ancient writer, and entitled

The Two Loves.

Two loves there are. I once knew one
　　Who came beneath the golden skies
　　　　With marvellous eyes.
Catching the splendour of the sun,
　　His finger touched me on the breast,
　　　　And left no rest.

Like, ah but unlike! He who came
Next with a song too gay and light,
A merry wight,
Had not the finger tipped with flame.
The day with him was mirthful mad;
The night too sad.

Come back again, young Love that first,
When blush on dainty lady-smocks
The maiden mocks,
So sudden sweet upon me burst!
Bring, to appease my wild desire,
That finger's fire.

The Marquis carried away with him the delicate music of the old madrigal-maker, full of minor touches and sudden changes. He dreamt thereof the long night through, wearied as he was by his adventure of the afternoon. Few men or women with imagination have not traced the echo of the day's doings in the vague visions of the night; new forms they take through the kaleidoscope of Dreamland, but those forms seem familiar. And dreams have not power over us when the vital force is not at its highest; then they come, often in a refreshing, but often also in a torturing form. The Marquis dreamt pleasantly; to him the melody of the canzonet repeated itself in countless ways; while Cis Englehurst was faintly visible to him in the many magical shapes which Mercutio ascribed to Queen Mab, and a thousand more, which even the facile fancy of Mercutio could not paint.

> " For unto every lover his own lady is
> All ladies and all beauties and all mysteries,
> The breathing multiple of roses passionate,
> Of perfect pearls, of birds with happy melody;
> Ay, a mere girl, yet in herself a universe."

As to Cecilia, for hours she slept not. She was questioning her heart, which just began to awaken. She opened her favourite poet, and read for the thousandth time

two lines which all at once seemed to have
a meaning which she had never guessed :—

> " But to her heart her heart was voluble,
> Paining with eloquence her balmy side."

The magic scene which the young poet
depicted with felicity of phrase almost
Shakespearian, seemed to arise before her.
On her breast also, as on Madeline's, Love,
or the phantom of Love (which was it ?)
" threw warm gales," and when

> " Her rich attire creeps rustling to her knees,"

she wishes it were the eve of Saint
Agnes, and that she might see her real
lover, even as Madeline beheld Porphyro.
Have such things ever been ? Or is it
only the fond poet's dream ?

What chance, I wonder, had the hapless
Charles Cotton, away in London, in
Dulau's Soho lodging ? The young glazier

dreamt of Englehurst night after night;
dreamt of the young beauty he had beheld
when he put in that unforgettable pane of
glass; did not, however, dream that a new
mist of romance surrounded her. Poor
fellow! How could he expect to fight
with such fortune as that of the handsome
adventurous affluent Marquis? Pshaw!
Better, O Charles Cotton, forget your
daring family motto, forget lovely Cis
Englehurst, and settle down patiently to
regular plumber and glazier's work, and a
stout country girl for a wife.

Vain would it have been to give Charles
Cotton this clearly prudent advice. Amid
the unaccustomed distractions of London,
and with a mystery which for his own
sake he was fain to solve, the darling
dream was in his heart. The charm of

Cecilia Englehurst was written on the retina of his brain, as the picture of the home of his youth, with its white jessamine and sweet honeysuckle, is inscribed on the mind of the returning voyager who has spent long years in strange countries and among wild people. Verily, without imagination, man is man no longer. That supposititious wanderer may not find the old cottage of his childhood overhung with creepers; may not meet the recognising eyes of a single friend of his youth. But he has the delicious vision. And so Cotton, whether ever again he might come nigh the lady of his fantasy, was able to dwell in ceaseless thought upon eyes like living gems under casket-lids of rose-flushed ivory, on her mouth like a bud which love would turn to a flower, upon the lissom beauty of her movement, the dainty grace that was her own alone.

Morning came, a joyous autumnal dawn; not very joyous indeed to poor Charles Cotton in Soho, but he was true to his motto, " In utraque fortuna paratus," and he bore his dull life well enough. Dull it was, though Dulau in his own way tried to find amusement for a guest whom he highly honoured, as being commended to him by the Marquis. On this particular day Cotton arose early, felt the stuffy air of Soho too much for him, and wandered away westward. A market-gardener's empty two-horse waggon came trotting along from Covent Garden; the driver, a jolly-looking fellow, who had just breakfasted on beef and beer, after delivering

his master's wares to his salesman, shouted
to Cotton, asking him whether he would
like a lift. It was in Kensington High
Street, and Cotton was pining for country
air, so he sprang up on the seat of the
waggon. The carman was a pleasant fellow, who liked his glass of stout, and knew
where the barmaids were prettiest. What
wonder if the horses were stopped in the
Broadway at Hammersmith, at the Pigeons
at Brentford, at the Rose and Crown at
Hounslow, at the Magpies four miles farther on ?

The nursery gardens were close to
Bedfont, the legend of whose two peacocks Tom Hood has given us in octave
rhyme, in his least felicitous style ; and,
notwithstanding the frequent stoppages in
honour of Barclay and Perkins, saints at

whose shrine Cotton never before had so freely worshipped, the fast trotting horses reached here at about seven o'clock. Just as they were pulling up, the scream of a traction engine frightened them ; the driver, who was in a careless mood, was taken by surprise; they bolted and upset the light waggon into a ditch, and Cotton was thrown right over the low hedge into the nursery grounds. He had no bones broken, by good hap, but was sorely shaken. The driver alighted on his skull, which, being the toughest portion of his person, saved him from utter destruction.

Cotton found himself in the very midst of an asparagus bed, which he had seriously damaged. The driver was not hurt a bit, having taken sufficient stout to deprive him of the resisting power

which makes an accident dangerous.
Harm seldom happens to a drunken
man.

When Cotton recovered from his shock,
and began to realise his position, a quaint-
looking girl of about sixteen was looking
at him, with commiserating eyes.

"Are you hurt much?" she said. "I
was obliged to laugh when I saw you
thrown over Papa's hedge; but I cried
after, because I thought you must be
killed."

"I don't think I'm hurt at all," said
Cotton, stretching himself to ascertain
whether his physical machinery was
in good order. "Have I committed a
dreadful trespass?"

"O no," she said. "You must come in
and see Papa. He encourages trespassers,

because he says they buy his flowers and fruit. Come along."

Cotton followed this gay short-frocked maiden, much amused. Presently two others, younger sisters, came dancing down to meet them. They were all three alike, with short curly brown hair, and noses of the *retroussé* style, and mouths a trifle too large, and ancles a trifle too thick.

" There are my sisters," said the elder maiden. " I am Hyacinth, and this is Ixia, and the little chit is Anemone. Papa names us all with flowers' names."

" A very pretty way of christening," said Cotton.

They went up a long gravel walk with espaliers on each side, and reached the house, a thatched cottage, smothered in

Virginia creeper, wistaria, honeysuckle, and many another clematis. In its low rustic porch sat a stalwart man of fifty, with a book in his hand, and a strangely uncertain look in his wide open eyes. He rose as his daughter came with Cotton to the door: and from within a lady came forward, imperially tall, who seemed as if she were mistress of all around her.

"Mamma!" whispered Hyacinth, and by immediate intuition Cotton knew that this meant "step-mamma!" No *injusta noverca* this; but . . . .

"You are welcome, sir," she said, in a voice so musical that its sound was like a song. "My husband is glad to welcome you or any other stranger, although he cannot see you."

"No," said the master of the house, "a

flash of lightning cost me my eyesight.
But speak, and I shall know what you are
like. Is not that so, Perdita?"

CHAPTER VI

THE MARKET GARDEN.

RAPHAEL.—I am adventurous, who would fain be indolent.

ASTROLOGOS.—Venus and Mars conjunct at your nativity
Gave love of luxury, with power of princeliness ;
With you, my lord, 'tis always fight or festival.
The Comedy of Dreams.

CHARLES COTTON began to think he was fated to meet with adventures. His first ride in a Covent Garden waggon had landed him in an asparagus bed, and he felt in quite a dream as he saw the blind gardener, his stately wife, the three little flower-christened girls. His idea of

London had never been poetic, or even romantic; he thought of it as a place where unpleasant people did unpleasant work for money. He would have liked to put panes of glass into manorial windows all his life, especially if through those " magic casements" he could see perpetual visions of Cis Englehurst. He was embarrassed and puzzled by the mighty fulness of London, its vast variety, its grandeur and horror. New types of character came under his eyes so frequently that he began to realise the thought that, when God made the race of man, He made a race of infinite possibility. Charles Cotton had studied no science, but he had a clear brain and a poetic instinct; and what he saw of London stimulated him to a higher view of humanity than that which village life could ever give. It may be said that Bedfont is not London, and that is topographically true, but not psychologically. London's suburbs stretch far into England. Is not Brighton what Thackeray called it —London-super-Mare ? A meagre borrower has called it Piccadilly-super-Mare—as if the four miles of shops, hotels, clubs, mansions, lodging-houses, which stretch along the Brighton shore, could be compared with the classic street in which Palmerston has lounged, of which Locker has sung.

When a man is told to speak, so that you may judge of his character, he is decidedly under a disadvantage, especially if he is an unsophisticated villager, like Cotton. But the lady who had been called Perdita, and who looked at the

young man with an air of grave amusement
which almost awed him, said, in her
strangely musical voice,

" In this garden we are beyond the roar
of the world, so what you say will not be
deadened by that external tumult."

" I have nothing to say," he replied,
" except that I hardly know how I came
here, and that I am glad to be here."

" He is six feet high," said the blind
gardener, as to himself, " with curly brown
hair, blue eyes, and a confoundedly long
nose. He will either turn out a devilish
good fellow, or go straight down hill to
the devil."

Hyacinth and Ixia and Anemone, accustomed to their father's oracular sayings,
laughed pleasantly, but were silenced by
their stately step-mother's uplifted finger,

and stood like pretty little statues. Her least look magnetised them. The gardener went on :

"Come, let us be festive. I have got a listener, I can perceive, so let us entertain him well. Find a melon, Hyacinth ; and, Ixia, look for figs; and, Anemone, see if there are nectarines left. Perdita, some sparkling wine. Our guest was not brought roughly into our garden without some sufficient reason: meet it is that we entertain him."

Everyone obeyed orders, and in five minutes a dainty service of fruit and wine, as delicate as that which Eve set before the "affable archangel," stood glistening in the porch, the three flower-maidens standing ready to wait. The melon was no larger than a cricket-ball, and dark green as to rind, and its fresh cut pink, fine, and juicy; the figs were purple and moist, untouched by hornet or wasp; the nectarines, delicately sunburnt, had a flavour incomparable. The wine sparkled in fanciful goblets. Neither Perdita nor the children partook of this poetic refection.

Cotton, amused and puzzled, enjoyed it. Presently the gardener said, "Children, go." Whereat the girls ran away at once; and then added, "Perdita, I want to talk to our friend. Lead me to the balcony."

She obeyed in a splendid fashion, as if she were a royal slave, a Cleopatra obeying a blind Cæsar. Taking his arm she led him up a wide stairway for so small a cottage, and he was seated in an old oak chair. Cotton also found a seat in the balcony, from which there was a lovely view of the fragrant and fertile garden.

"You can leave us, Perdita," he said, and she went without a word. Yet as she swept by Cotton seemed to perceive a touch of defiance in her stately movement.

"Listen, young man," said the gardener. "I heard your voice and liked it, and I want to say my say to somebody. You can see women obey me, and I generally make men do it. I've had a queer life. When I was a young fool I got entangled with my mother's lady's-maid—it's a deuced easy entanglement, young fellow, I can tell you. Don't you try it."

"I haven't got a mother," said Cotton, "and if I had she wouldn't have a lady's-maid."

"They're a queer race," said the gardener, reflectively. " I ought to have known better than to have been taken in, for I was past thirty, and she was a dumpy little animal with a vile temper. However, I married her, and my father—he was a stockbroker, and wanted to found a family —left all his money to a lot of hospitals. I didn't care. I had a few thousands, and I turned gardener. My wife was a bore, illiterate and ill-tempered, so I just treated her like a slave. She gave me three daughters, and I gave them flower-names, but they are not much like flowers; they've inherited their mother's ugliness and dulness, but not her ill temper, I'm glad to say. That's partly because I gave them over to the crossest German governess I could get, with special orders for severe castigation on the least occasion. But I suppose they in some degree inherit my own serenity of temper."

Charles Cotton was of course delighted with that supposition.

"Well, they are the three little jades, and I don't know what I shall do with them. They'd make capital gardeners' wives. You're not a gardener, I can see, else you might have one—or all three for that matter. Those girls do good work. I turn them out at five in summer, and six in winter, and I'll back them against any three men in my employ for all but rough business."

"They must get very tired," said Cotton.

"Of course they do, and a good thing for them. They come in at six, have supper at seven, and are in bed at eight, with all lights out. They're happy enough. Don't they seem so to you?"

Cotton admitted that they did.

"Yes, you are right," said the gardener. "Inferior animals need hard work, and my poor wife was a very inferior animal, and the girls follow her. It can't be helped."

He paused awhile. Cotton was satisfied to look across the pleasant garden to where Hyacinth and Ixia were up lofty ladders, picking ribstone pippins, looking in the distance more like wood-nymphs. Anemone was invisible, busy in the mushroom house.

"I feel garrulous to-day," said the gardener; "garrulous as Nestor. I daresay you will forget my story. You saw Perdita?"

"The lady who is your wife?" said Cotton.

"She is not my wife, though I allow the girls to think so—nor is she my mistress, though she is with me day and night. She is my faithful friend. You will deem it strange that I have never seen her face, and that I do not know her name."

"It is strange," said Cotton.

"You shall hear. Just after little Anemone was born, at which time her mother died, I was down at my front gate about midnight, in the midst of a tremendous thunderstorm. I love the grand roll of thunder; and when I could see the clouds exchanging sheets of flame, or the fierce forked zigzags falling in triple lines from sky to earth, I seemed to become an elemental soul. That night I saw the last of lightning. A carriage and four, the horses frightened by the storm, was dashed against my gate-posts. I ran out, in time to take a lady in a fainting state from the coach, but the lightning at the very moment blinded me, as she lay in my arms. How it did not kill me I cannot guess. I know nothing of what followed, except that I carried her from the gate to the house, where everybody was in bed, and groped my way upstairs with her. I was dizzy with the frightful shock. Only the strong impulse of having a life to save could have brought me so far. I put her on the bed, and then I sank beside her, absolutely unable to do more. And the next thing I remember is the feeling of her soft hand upon my brow, hours afterwards, bathing it with some fragrant water."

"A marvellous incident," said Cotton.

"I have related it to no one but you," said the gardener, "and I desire no one else to know it. I felt compelled to speak, like the Ancient Mariner of Coleridge. Perdita has been with me ever since, and has shown infinite gratitude and faithfulness. I have never asked her a question. I have elsewhere learnt that she was at that moment, when Jupiter Tonans and I interfered, running away from her husband with some other man, and that her husband is a person of some importance, and wonders very much what can have become of her. Do you consider her handsome?"

"Superbly so," said Cotton.

"Ah, and I shall never see her. So much the better, perhaps. She is a good creature, in her limited way."

"You have no strong affection for her, then?" said Cotton. "Her beauty would intoxicate many men."

"That fountain of intoxication is closed for me; and I could never love a woman who for one instant had cared for another man."

"Yet you accept her kindly service, and allow your daughters to think her your wife. I am only a boy, and have not read much on such subjects, but I should think two persons living together in that way could scarcely be happy."

"Did I say I was happy, young man? Did I say she was happy? Think out both cases. Can you imagine me happy, with a certainty that never more shall my old eyes behold sky or sea or land?"

"Homer and Milton were blind," said Cotton.

"I am not a poet. The physical eye is outdone by the imagination. Homer saw the gods on Olympus, and Milton saw Adam with Eve in Eden, while the defeated Archangel watched to betray them. I have no such visions to console me, and long to see even so commonplace a thing as a bed of lettuces. And I admit that I would give anything to see Perdita."

He paused a few moments, while Cotton sat silent, and then went on again.

"That she should be happy is, of course, absurd. She did a great misdeed, which, but for an accident, might have been greater. The sudden shock of that thunderstorm brought her in some measure to her right mind. I believe the man from whom she fled was a villain, and of course the man with whom she was flying was a thorough villain. I think over the matter perpetually, and construct all sorts of theories about her, and I have come to this conclusion. She is a lady whom the brutality of a bad husband drove into the arms of a worse lover. Rescued from both by an unparalleled incident, she determines to keep aloof from both, and makes a vow to do all that she can for me, her chance rescuer. That is my idea, and with that idea I accept her services, treating her as my equal, but expecting obedience."

"That man has a taste for tyranny," thought Cotton, but he quite agreed with his theory.

"Let us walk round the garden," said the gardener. "You will not object to give me your arm."

They loitered through it, and in noble order it was for the season of the year. Cotton noted that when they approached any man at work he accelerated his pace even more promptly than even if his master had been a man unsmitten by blindness. The gardener seemed to know by some new sense the condition of all the various beds and houses, and often remarked on them in words so apposite that Cotton was quite amazed at what seemed like divination.

"How are your mushrooms, Anemone?" he said, as they looked in upon the long lines of shelves where they were growing white as snow.

The child, by way of reply, brought him a perfect specimen, with a lovely pink blush on its under side; and the gardener said :—

"Send up some of the choicest. This gentleman will stay to dine."

"I ought to go back to London," said Cotton. "I do not think I can stay to dine."

The gardener laughed.

"O yes you can. You were thrown over my hedge for some real purpose, depend on .it. It must be divined at least. It may be something which you dream not of."

Cotton felt quite disposed to see his adventure to its end, and readily gave way. They had a long lounge through the gardens, which were of great extent, and capitally kept. " Oculus domini saginat equum," says a well-known Latin adage; but in this case it was manifestly not the master's eye, but the master's pre-

sence, which did the business. He was
surprised to see that a man without eyesight could thus control a difficult business.

Cotton, who was only too glad of
something to occupy him, enjoyed his
wandering through these gardens, enjoyed
also the quaint gardener's most eccentric
talk, and felt on the whole thankful that
he had been thrown over a hedge into an
asparagus bed and odd company. Many
curious occurrences amused him in the
course of the day. There was a carriage-
drive right through the nursery, so that
any visitors might come close to the chief
conservatories; and in the afternoon a
good many visitors came. By this time
Hyacinth and Ixia had given up their out-
door work, and were busy manufacturing

exquisite tiny bouquets for male button-
holes, and splendid flower-fancies for female
hands to hold. It was pretty to see them.
The gardener found himself with much to
do, for he always looked after his important
customers. So Charles Cotton, after watching with much amusement the way in
which swells paid their button-hole half-
crowns and their guineas for ladies' bouquets, strolled away by himself, carrying
the thought in his brain that, as money
must be wasted, it may be wasted on worse
things than flowers.

Wandering thus in a part of the grounds
away from the great conservatories, he
came suddenly upon little Anemone, who
was busily picking herbs. She looked up
with a merry smile, and said,

"These are for something or other

mamma is making for your dinner. Come
and see what she is going to do with
them."

Cotton went with the little girl, and at
the old-fashioned kitchen porch, covered
with creepers, was greeted by Perdita,
who chanced to be waiting for these same
herbs. She had covered herself with a
cook's apron, and stood there in the
afternoon sunlight just like a cook in a
comedy. She made Cotton a very elegant
mock curtsey, and said,

"This young hussy has kept me waiting
for the herbs I wanted; but I trust you
will like your dinner, sir."

Yes, there she was, in the quaint cottage
kitchen, cooking the dinner, with no help
but that of little Anemone ; and the kitchen,
to Charles Cotton, seemed ennobled by her

presence, and she looked to him like a goddess who was cooking a dinner for fun.

"Now," she said, "I am sure you are hungry, wandering about those gardens with the Master. He never gets tired, but he tires other people. Sit down and have some soup in a homely way."

So Cotton sat down to the deal kitchen table, and very much enjoyed the plate of soup set before him on the instant—which was not remarkable, since good gravy-beef furnished the foundation, while oysters and celery gave it flavour. And the cook found him a glass of wine too—excellent Bucellas.

"Now tell me," said Perdita, looking at Cotton with a strange smile, "which do you take to be the oddest person—the

Master or I ?   He has told you our story,
I am certain.   I saw he meant to; he
needed some one to confide it to.   Whatever he has told you is true, for he could
not lie.   He has never asked me who I
am; I believe he has never tried to guess.
And it really does not matter; I am only
a silly woman, who was arrested by what
seems a miraculous accident on the brink
of a downward career, which must have
ended horribly.   You see I speak frankly."

"But this must be a happy life," said
Cotton, who could not help feeling the
idyllic beauty of the calm garden, with its
regular succession of work.   The great
conservatories blazed in the sunshine,
sheets of radiant hyaline with masses of
many-coloured bloom beneath.   They
looked as changeful under the shifting

light as Love's versicoloured wings, described by Virgil, *Catalecta* vi. 9. It
seemed to him that nothing could be more
charming than such an existence.

"Happiness," said Perdita, "is the crea- .
ture of the mind. I feel content : but to
be happy there must be no ugly blot on
the memory, no haunting ghost of a past
remorse. I don't know," she said, with a
smile, "why I talk in this way to you, a
youthful stranger, except indeed that I
know the Master has been telling you the
curious tale. I am quiet here ; I am glad
to serve him ; I like those quaint three
daughters of mine ; I like the fruit, the
flowers, the tranquil life. But the past is
eternal."

I should say that Perdita looked more
like Mrs. Siddons as a cook of tragedy

than anything else. But Cotton knew
nothing of Mrs. Siddons, and he felt that
he was in the presence of a very wonderful
woman. Devoid till quite lately of any
experience of the great world, he was
slightly bewildered. He thought to himself that it would be rather pleasant to
live in such a place, and mend the glass of
the conservatories and the pipes of the
hot-water apparatus. Very delightful!
Only he couldn't live anywhere without
Cis Englehurst.

"Well, I must return to my cooking,"
she said. "I hope you will find amusement till dinner-time."

"No fear," he answered. "This garden
is inexhaustible."

He wandered away through its laby-
rinthine avenues, and enjoyed the time.

At intervals he came across little Anemone, who was occupied in multitudinous
divisions of business. He was amused at
this little garden-fairy, who, withal her
petit nez retroussé, was a nice specimen of
the modern hamadryad.

The dinner was to be at six, and notwithstanding the flavorous basin of soup
which he had received at the imperial Perdita's fair hands, Cotton's healthy appetite
began to feel renewal. Healthy hunger is
among the most fortunate faculties of
youth. When you no longer enjoy your
bread and cheese and beer, my reader,
consider there is something wrong; perchance you are overfagged, or overnagged
by a cantankerous wife, or do not work
your brain and your muscle enough. We
are the victims of overwork and under-

work. Society is so disorganised that some men are always overworked, and they wither away into mere atomies; and some are underworked, and they get as fat as an old lady's pug dog; and few, ah, how few! get exactly the amount of work which is good for them, or the kind which, they can do best. I will say this for Charles Cotton—he would gladly have put in panes of glass for the remainder of his life, if only through each pane he could see the lovely face of Cecilia Englehurst.

Dinner time arrived, and the gardener and his guest sat down to a pleasant meal, which I will not describe, (1) because I am accused of such descriptions too often; and the *Spectator* declared, when criticising my "Seven Village Songs" in *Blackwood*, that no other man had ever dared to put a cutlet into a love-lyric; (2) because that dinner never came to an end, and Anemone's choicest mushrooms were spoilt. Just as Perdita, with her air of regal servitude, had set the first dish on the table, and retreated to the kitchen for its accessories, there came a fierce flash of lightning, striking like the sword of an archangel across the open window. The gardener saw it not; but in a few seconds came a reverberating peal of thunder, which made him spring to his feet, just as Perdita re-entered the room. He went straight to the open window and faced the sky.

"Lightning and thunder drive him wild," whispered Perdita. "He has a mad thought that, as a thunderstorm destroyed his eyesight, a thunderstorm may

restore it. Keep near him, for my sake; I
dare not speak to him now."

So Cotton went to the window and
looked at the storm. It was one of those
storms for which London is famous. The
mighty cities of the earth draw down the
mighty storms of the sky. The gardener
stood there, rapt; striving to gaze into
the infinite black depths of space; striving
to see lightning. He saw it not. His
blank eyeballs refused to perceive the
Promethean fire. Yet it crossed the sky
in lines which seemed as if they would
cut the firmament in two, and set the
world alight.

This was the vanguard of the glorious
storm; the cavalry of light which moved
fiercely to the front. Then came a huge
and heavy bank of clouds, a park of

heaven's artillery. The gardener heard the mighty thunder-claps; he could not see the lightning, and that saddened him.

"Oh," he cried, "if only I could see lightning again!"

As he spoke, there came a swift zigzag flash and loud thunder the instant after. And then, hail! It fell, formed by the electric force in thunderclouds, with great swiftness; the ground was in a moment white with it. The stones were some as large as pigeon's eggs. They could hear them from the window where they stood crashing into the conservatories as if they were Prussian artillery.

"I shan't have a pane of glass left to-morrow," said the gardener.

"How lucky that I am a glazier!" said Charles Cotton.

CHAPTER VII.

AFTER THE STORM.

ASTROLOGOS.—Nothing is half so glorious as a thunderstorm.
ALOUETTE.—O yes, papa, a thunderstorm is exquisite,
    If you have only some one's arm around your waist.
                                    The Comedy of Dreams.

THE gardener's night was an excited
one. The influx of a tremendous
tempest of hail is a terrible matter for a
garden with half an acre of glass. He
and Cotton and his men went out to dis-
cover what could be done, but blinding
showers of heavy hail descended, and they
were absolutely driven back and routed.

The most famous poetic gardener of the day wrote to me a year or two ago, saying that an army of wasps, led by a generalissimo in the shape of an enormous hornet, had fairly driven him out of his orchard house. That was a trifle to the advent of this destructive hail, which crashed through multitudinous panes of glass, cut up vines and flowers, and did infinite damage.

" Nothing can be done," said the gardener. " Send the girls to bed, Perdita."

" O no, no, please not, dear papa," said little Anemone. "I could not sleep. I should be quite miserable in bed."

" Well," said the gardener to Charles Cotton, " do you feel disposed to stay up awhile and watch the storm? It will roar itself out at midnight, I prophesy, and leave me without a pane of glass or a Mus-

cat grape. What matter? I have always
been the sport of fortune. Jupiter Pluvius
is to me no novelty. Perdita, as we have
not dined, let us have something devilled,
and brew a bowl of punch, and we will try
to imagine we are happy."

There was a pleasant midnight. Perdita
lighted a fire with logs of young ash—

> " Ash when green
> Is fire for a queen—"

and the three children set to work to give
help, which help they gave dexterously. A
silver gridiron was placed on the fire, with
a splendid young capon spaich-cocked upon
it; and little Hyacinth knelt down and
cooked slices of bacon on a toasting fork
till her pretty face was abnormally hot and
red. All the while the gardener and
Charles Cotton were calmly smoking cigars.

All the while the hail was descending in a deluge, and the roof gave token of its fall, and there was crash of glass till it seemed no glass was left to be crashed. All the while the lightning flashed so fiercely that it seemed as if the heavy curtains must take fire—the thunder reverberated so loudly that they could hardly hear each other speak.

Charles Cotton, having a tendency to study human nature, was much amused with his company. The despotic gardener, the imperial and imperious Perdita, were well worth study. He, lying back in his easy chair, with blinded eyes, listened to the elemental roar, and wondered what strange destruction would meet other eyes to-morrow. She, knowing well that he, the gardener, was after all more important

than all the glass in his greenhouse, took
the greatest care to make him comfortable,
and brewed his punch with as much care
as she browned the legs of his capon, all
piquant with French mustard and Nepaul
pepper. Cotton, watching her, wondered
much at her. She might have been a queen,
and chose to be a slave.

Great fun was it for Hyacinth and Ixia
and Anemone to be up half the night because
the greenhouses were smashed by a hail-
storm. These young things don't know
what money trouble means. Why should
they? It was for them just a period of
excitement; the fragments of capon and
bacon and cinnamon in punch delighted
them; above all, they were to sit up. When
I was a boy I have had to sit up all night
for the purpose of travelling by a mail

coach that started at four or five in the morning. I am no longer a boy, and I certainly should not do it now. But to children who usually go to bed at eight the notion of a late night is perfectly delightful, and these three girls were so excited that at intervals Perdita was compelled to calm them.

Soon after midnight, as the gardener had predicted, the storm had roared itself away. The thunder grew fainter and fainter, like the artillery of a retreating army. The three girls were by this time fast asleep on a large red velvet sofa which stood by the fire—a quaint group of happy sleepers, whose apparel was not so well ordered, nor their *pose* so artistic, as those of Tennyson's Sleeping Beauty. One after the other had given way to our old friend

Morpheus, the god of many forms. Little
Anemone was the last to drop soft lids
over drowsy childish eyes. Perhaps this
child, named from the windflower, had
stronger sympathy with the winds than
her elder sisters. Charles Cotton said
something of the kind to the gardener, as
he watched them falling asleep one after
the other, and his host agreed with him.

"I have always held," he said, "that
Christian names have something to do
with destiny, where the creature christened
hath a sensitive soul. Every Emily is a
flirt, and every Mary Ann, or Sarah Jane,
a born maid-servant. You may say that
my daughters have Pagan rather than
Christian names. At any rate, they all
have meaning. Now I had no classic
right to call that elder child Hyacinth,

since Hyacinthus was a boy. When play-
ing quoits with Apollo, jealous Zephyrus
threw a quoit in such a way as to kill the
handsome youth. 'Tis only the way the
Greeks had of expressing natural truths.
A hyacinth caught by the wind when the
sun is on it must surely die. Well, my
little Hyacinth justified her baptism, for
she is a regular little tomboy; and I
believe she made acquaintance with you
not at all shyly."

"She was uncommonly kind," said
Cotton. "I owe to her a most pleasant
day, and a night even pleasanter."

Perdita said nothing, but she looked
quite gratefully at Cotton, for her greatest
delight in life was to make her rescuer
happy.

"A pleasant night without any sleep,"

said the gardener. " Tobacco instead of dreams."

" A fortunate substitute now and then," said Cotton. " Dreams form upon the smoke wreaths ; once or twice to-night the white vapour rose in air like a lovely lady whom I have seen dressed in white."

Perdita smiled.

" Ha! in love, my friend. You begin early. But now for names. Little Ixia is named from the chameleon-plant, which changes colour according to its soil, and a most changeable child she is. One day she is as good as gold, and another as mischievous as a monkey. She has to be kissed in the morning and whipped in the afternoon. And as to Anemone, she is, you see, a lover of the winds."

As they talked the storm retreated, and

they went to the front door. The heavy
black clouds had passed away, and a bright
full moon was in the zenith. The water
was still running down the gravel paths;
the plants looked drenched and miserable;
great gaps could be seen in the greenhouse
glass. It was a strange scene.

As they stood silently looking at the
moon, a shadow touched its rim.

"What is that?" said Cotton. "Not a
cloud."

"The shadow of the earth," said Perdita.
"There is an eclipse of the moon to-night.
The storm caused me to forget it."

"I have never seen an eclipse," said
Cotton.

"I shall never see another," observed
the gardener; "but I well remember when
I was a schoolboy being delighted to sit

up all night and watch one. The fact is fixed on my mind because a tame jackdaw that I kept took the opportunity to drown himself. He was anti-astronomical, I expect. They make a great fuss about eclipses, these astronomers; but after all it is, as Perdita says, merely the passing of a shadow. There is a fine couplet of Shelley's :—

'As when some great painter dips
His pencil in the hues of earthquake and eclipse.'"

"I have never read Shelley," said Cotton.

"A man who has never seen an eclipse or read Shelley is a black swan. What have you done, my friend?"

"Put in many panes of glass in my time, so that perhaps to-morrow I may be of some use to you."

"Thanks," said the gardener; "I will with pleasure accept your aid. I wonder if there could by any chance be a connexion between the eclipse and the thunderstorm? The old historians connected earthquakes and comets with unusual events. If they were right—and I am not prepared to say they were not—I look forward to the year 1897."

"Why?" asked Cotton.

"Because there will be no eclipses either of the sun or moon."

"Let us hope we shall reach that miraculous year," replied Cotton.

By this time the moon's silver disc was completely obscured by the shadow of our fast-flying planet, which travels so swiftly that we cannot perceive her movement— her pace being between sixteen and seventeen miles a second, or about sixty thousand miles an hour. Few people realise this rapid travel; even as few people know that the music of the spheres is in so high a key as to be inaudible to mortal ears.

The moon was now entirely obscure. Cotton reported progress to the gardener. Perdita spoke little; the beauty of this sky movement seemed to render her more silent than usual, silent as she always was. The great trouble and terror of her life had driven back into her heart the natural fresh feelings of a woman in her prime; and her chief thought was to enslave herself willingly to her rescuer, whom she regarded much as a heathen regarded his own special patron among the gods of his pantheon. Remorse and gratitude mingled; admiration for him, and contempt for the two villains who caused her disgrace—these were her perpetual spur to action. That he should have lost his eyesight at such a moment, to save her from dishonour—he to whom the light of the sun was a divine delight—and that he should never say a discontented word, was to her an endless pain. What could she do for him but humbly serve? He could not love her, she knew, for he could love no woman who had done what she had done. And his tyranny was very pleasant. He *would* have his way. Even before the days of Petruchio it was pretty well known that women like a man who *will* have his way.

The shadow of the earth began to leave the moon.

"Let us go to bed, Perdita," said the gardener. "Let us snatch an hour or two of sleep before sunrise. Leave the children on their sofa; it would be a shame to wake them. Show Mr. Cotton his room."

When Charles Cotton awoke next morning, which was about five, he beheld a delightful autumnal day, with not a breath of trouble in the air. He got down and out into the gardens before the gardener rose. He looked at the conservatories, and saw there had been desperate damage from the merciless hail. He found out the nearest glazier, got a shelf of glass and some putty, and was soon up a ladder, putting in glass with a dexterous hand. When the gardener came out he would not stop for breakfast, and would

only interrupt himself to drink a glass of
bitter ale, handed up to him on his
ladder. He worked all day with great
resolve. The three flower-christened girls
aided him, bringing him the various materials of his trade as he needed them, and
being indeed almost too eager to help.
There was Hyacinth with glass, and Ixia
with putty, and Anemone with anything
she could find. And then, as he refused
to go into the house for lunch, seeing that
he was in the middle of work, Perdita
brought him a basin of soup and some
sherry, which he took very comfortably on
his ladder, then returning to his work.

Charles Cotton had never in his life put
in so many panes of glass as he put in that
day. It was a thorough piece of hard
work. When it was over he was con-

foundedly tired. He made his final descent from the oft-moved ladder, feeling
that he had got through the worst of his
work. As he descended, Hyacinth (who
had hardly for a moment deserted him)
was there to receive him : he was cramped
by working all day in an unusual position,
and the little tomboy offered him her arm,
and piloted him home with much kindness.
A good girl, Hyacinth. Yet! Well, she
could not help liking Charles Cotton a
trifle too much—which is very improper
for your girls of sixteen? and he somehow
could not help seeing it in her tell-tale
eyes ; and then he thought of Cis Englehurst. Hyacinth was a nice little garden
flower. Cis was a goddess—to Cotton,
any way. Ah me, that magic casement!
That pane of glass which brought the
pain of love !

Strange! As he and Hyacinth went
down the garden path to the cottage, there
stood a carriage and pair in front of one
of the conservatories, and in that carriage
indolently lounged the Marquis de Castelcicala. No mistaking that handsome
Italian. He was in a reverie. His companion, whoever that companion might
have been, had gone into the conservatory.
He had manifestly not been interested
enough to follow her—for of course it was
a *her*. As Cotton and Hyacinth passed,
he chanced to see them, descended from
the carriage, and said,

"I did not expect to see you here.
Wait a few moments. I want to talk to
you."

The Marquis went into the conservatory. He paid a courteous adieu to the

lady with whom he had come down, telling
her that an accident rendered it impossible
for him to return with her to Park Lane.
As it had been an accidental meeting, an
accidental parting was its natural *sequitur*.

Then he strolled down between the
espaliers to where Hyacinth, a funny little
espiègle flower, was loitering with Cotton.

"Odd that I should be here, Cotton," he
said. "Please introduce me to this
charming young lady."

"Her name is Hyacinth," said Cotton.

"The goddess Flora named her," said
the Marquis. "I came here with a lady
whom I know very slightly, and who
wanted to buy a bouquet of some greenhouse flowers. I have shaken myself free
of her since. She is a casual acquaintance, whom I am only compelled to know

by reason of etiquette. Hence I was glad of an excuse to talk with you. I came up from Erlingham because we have a little further information; but the Squire is getting tired of the whole business. He wants to buy Miss Cecilia some more diamonds, and make her forget the others were stolen. I dare say it would be the wiser plan."

"If a thief can be found, punish that thief," said Cotton. "What do you say, Hyacinth?"

"Where hyacinths grow there will be thieves," said the Marquis. "The prettiest flowers are the soonest stolen. For my own part I prefer a hyacinth to a diamond."

Hyacinth, a rustic maiden unaccustomed to such courtliness of speech, blushed a little as the Marquis spoke. She was puzzled, as well she might be, 'twixt Cotton and Castelcicala. They were both unintelligible folk to this little nymph of the garden. She liked them both, but she could not understand them; and when a woman cannot understand a man, she is apt to draw an entirely inaccurate picture of him.

The result was that they walked round the garden, and enjoyed it much. Castelcicala had never before seen a splendid English nursery ground, such as no other country can produce. You cannot grow a melon or a peach, a pineapple or a nectarine, out of England, even in the Orient realms wherein those delicious fruits were invented. It was wondrous to see the gardener's muscat grapes, of both colours, hanging from the glass roof—his peaches grown upon trees in pots, and ripening for dessert. The Marquis enjoyed all this; but as a student of character, he even more enjoyed little Hyacinth, a child who had grown to sixteen amid fruit and flowers. She was just a flower. A simple girl-flower, who loved other flowers. A boy-girl, her father averred; but with no atom of harm in her.

After wandering through the grounds, and witnessing the dilapidations, they came down towards the house. There everything was quiet. The gardener himself, after making a visitation of his whole demesne, had settled down in his easy-chair, feeling abominably tired. Ixia and Anemone were quite alive, and welcomed Hyacinth and the Marquis delightedly.

Perdita, the queenly Martha of the household, on hospitable cares intent, was not at the moment visible.

A very few words put the Marquis and the gardener *en rapport.* It is a matter to be remarked that the ethereal tincture of the soul is the same all through. A tailor or a cobbler who does his work well is on the same level as a general or statesman who does his work well. These two men understood each other instanter. And here were three men, an Italian marquis, an English gardener, and an English glazier, who got on well from the first. "What condescension in the Marquis!" says Boots de Boots, whose great grandfather was a waiter at Boodles'. I don't see it. I honour a good English workman as much as I honour a true English gentleman. Both are perfect in their kind. They are convertible. Cannot a gentleman be a workman, or a workman a gentleman?

They sat together and talked, the children quietly listening. The gardener would have no breach of discipline among his young folk. Hyacinth and Ixia and Anemone lived a happy life; but they had to work hard out of doors, and to obey their father and Perdita implicitly. They did it with the happy industry and obedience of love. They were good little rogues, who would in due time make excellent wives for somebody. I am thankful that it is not my present duty, as a novelist, to marry them.

"I came here by accident," said the Marquis, "with a lady whom I met by accident. Then I met my friend Cotton, who has been telling me how your thunder-storm cut you up, and that he had been able to help you, of which I was very glad. Then I met Miss Hyacinth, and thought what a lovely name she had. You have a most delightful corner here."

"It is well enough," said the gardener. "I try to be content. I can smell my roses and taste my nectarines; but I can see nothing. I cannot, indeed, see whether these little hussies of mine behave properly; but I know they are good girls."

They were all three around the blind old man's knees at that moment.

"Blind Thamyris and blind Maeonides,
And Tiresias, and Phineas, prophets old,"

were probably not unlike our friend the gardener. Knowledge at one entrance quite shut out, is extremely unsatisfactory;

but a good many blind men have been of
vast use in the world.   There is much to
be said for Homer and Milton.

It was well this night that the gardener
was blind.   His three flower-christened
children were crouching around his knees.
Cotton was sitting opposite.   The Marquis
de Castelcicala leant on the mantel-piece
on one arm.

Entered, pale and silent, Perdita.

Castelcicala *almost* went forward as if to
embrace her.   But he kept himself back,
saying under his breath—

"My God !   Impossible !"

CHAPTER VIII.

AMELIA'S IMPRISONMENT.

Sure, silliness is often worse than naughtiness,
Which in the long run gets the sharper punishment.

THAT Amelia Laing had not run away
with Charles Cotton we are aware.
As a fact, she had been driven wild by
her father and mother, and had thought of
doing something desperate. She was, however, saved the trouble. Mr. Laing, early
on the morning of the day when Cotton
and his daughter had so terribly shocked
his exquisite refinement by the scene in

the greenhouse, went to his daughter's room, and ordered her to dress, saying that he was about to take her to stay with a friend.

" I do not approve of your conduct with that young workman, Amelia," he said to the girl. "I intend you to go away for a time. Your mamma fully agrees with me. Dress at once, and let your maid pack a few things for you."

Amelia was only half awake. She could not help rejoicing at the thought of going anywhere for a change. Home was a weary imprisonment, with a perpetual quarrel on hand. The girl was a match for her father; but her mother would not allow her to defend her; and so this hoyden grew tired of her position, and dreamily welcomed anything for a change. She sprang out of bed and dressed rapidly, wondering the while whither she was destined to go. Gawky and awkward and dull though she was, there was the making of a fine woman, some day, in Amelia Laing. She was as true as her father was false, as brave as her mother was weak.

Mr. Laing got his daughter away that morning without the knowledge of her mother and the general household. The maid who waited on her was a little Irishwoman, very demure and sly, who was in his confidence, and acted under his orders. When Amelia told her to pack some things for her, she said,

" Why, Miss, are you going away?"

" Yes, Ella, for a day or two, I think. I shall be very glad of a change. I wish you were coming with me."

" I wish I was, Miss. I'm sure a change will do you good."

Laing had ordered the plausible minx to talk cheerfully to his daughter. Presently he came into her room and said,

" Don't disturb your mamma, Amelia ; she is fast asleep. There is a fly at the door, and Ella will take your bag down. I will ride over to the station. I have some letters to write. In case I am late, here is some money to take your ticket to London. I shall be there before the train starts, but you had better get into a carriage ; and, if I don't happen to be in the same, we shall meet at Paddington."

Thus it happened, through Laing's adroitness and Ella's connivance, that Amelia was supposed to have gone off by herself, with her pious parent hot in pursuit. This figment gathered strength from the fact that Mr. Laing took no leave of his wife; so that the weak woman, when she missed both father and daughter, was in a state of agonised wonderment. When she rang her bell, Ella answered it, with a sly look on her plausible face.

"Please, m'm," she said, "master told me to tell you he was gone to the station, and perhaps should have to go to London. He didn't want you disturbed. Miss Amelia's run away, and he's gone to find her."

"The wicked girl!" she said, shedding a torrent of tears. "To leave the best and kindest father that ever lived! O Ella, if you ever marry, I hope you'll get half as good a husband."

As Ella, being a perspicacious Irish lass, with full opportunity of judging Mr. Laing's character, did not quite agree in his wife's estimate, she only said,

" Yes, m'm, he *is* a gentleman, if there was ever a gentleman out of Ireland."

Laing got to the station just as the train was starting; indeed, he had purposely made it so close a thing that he had no time to take a ticket, and was obliged to pay at the end of his journey. His daughter, who had for once obeyed orders, saw him get into a carriage, and was satisfied. She had but one fellow-passenger, an elderly gentleman, who read the City article of the *Times* with intense care.

When they reached the terminus Mr. Laing greeted his daughter with unusual kindness. A brougham was ready, and they drove away. Amelia knew nothing of London. The crowded streets and multitudinous houses were a wonder to her, almost a terror. She had a dull, faint feeling, this girl, that she had something in her which wouldn't come out. She felt that she ought to understand many things which she could not understand, her father among the rest. Her eyes were wide open, I dare say her mouth also, as the brougham rapidly cut through London, and stopped at last at the gates of a very pleasant-looking villa on the Surrey side of the river.

The gates were opened. They drove up to the front of the house. The lawn and garden were charmingly kept. Amelia could not help exclaiming, " What a pretty place!" though she seldom said much to her father.

"Yes," he said, "and Mrs. Grimes is a charming old lady, and I think you will be sure to like the Misses Grimes."

Amelia had not heard these ineuphonious names before. She and her father were shown into a handsome drawing-room, where Mrs. Grimes and one of her daughters received them. The old lady was small, white-haired, with catlike eyes; indeed, Amelia at once thought she looked like a cat. The daughter was a tall girl, with a general look of power; her hair was light, her development Penthesilean. She might, as I have heard a small gentleman of my acquaintance say of his stalwart sweet-heart, have taken a man up and thrown him on to the roof of the house. I wonder these small gentlemen, so fond of giant wives, are not a little afraid of quasi-paternal discipline.

There was tea, and a chat, and presently Mr. Laing left, having business to do. He had, in fact, to face Crake, and extract money from that scoundrel by telling him a lie that he hoped might become truth. He saw possibilities in Amelia. Tall beyond the average height of woman, awkward by reason thereof, the child hardly knew what to do with herself. He now, under a false pretence, left her with Mrs. Grimes, an old lady who for years uncounted had made a fine income by turning hoydens and awkward giglots into young gentle-women. Poor Amelia had not the least idea where she was; she imagined merely a visit to a friend of her father's; she was amazed and horrified when old Mrs. Grimes (who looked uncommonly like a wicked old fairy) said, in a harsh voice,

" Susanna, let this child go to bed."

Susanna Grimes rang a bell : to Amelia's amazement it was answered by her old friend Jane Vincent, who, however, looked at her as if she had never seen her before in all her life. Amelia had sufficient presence of mind to take the cue. Miss Grimes said : " Miss Vincent, this is a new pupil. Let her sleep in your room to-night."

Amelia, who had not yet regarded herself as a pupil, was puzzled, and inwardly inclined to be rebellious. She was slow, you see, but she began to understand that her father had played her a cowardly trick. When she saw her old friend Jenny Vincent she kept quiet, though she felt a fierce passion against those who had conspired to place her in this position. She knew she was not too old to be at school; but she despised her father for the cowardly way in which he had carried out his design of placing her there. However, seeing her old friend, she was silent, and followed her without a word. She was led to a very comfortable double-bedded room.

"How *did* you come here?" said Jenny Vincent. "Whisper, dear; no talking is allowed."

"How did *you* come here?" she retaliated.

"O, I am a governess, you know. It is a capital place, and I get good pay. But, now, tell me why you are here."

"Papa never told me it was a school, or

anything. He said he wanted me to have a change, and would take me to visit a friend. And it *is* a school, is it, Jenny?"

"Yes, you dear little stupid, it is. It is a school specially intended for naughty girls, or, as Mrs. Grimes puts it in her prospectus, for young ladies of the patrician classes unfortunately endowed with ungovernable idiosyncrasies. Now, I don't know, of course, what your dear amiable father has said of you, but that old Grimes is a thoroughly cruel cat, so you had better make up your mind to be a very good girl indeed. She has many quaint devices in punishment, and her daughters are almost as clever as she is."

"How lucky I was to find you here, Jenny dear! I begin to hate papa. He might be honest."

"My dear old father, who made his living by selling newspapers, used to say that it was very hard to be honest now-a-day, if you wished to live. Still, I think he was straight enough. Now I mean to be dishonest to-night. I am ordered to make you generally uncomfortable, but I won't, for I know you don't deserve it. *Have* you been doing anything very dreadful lately?"

"Well, there was a glazier at work in the greenhouse, and he fell off a ladder and hurt himself, and I asked cook to give him some brandy, and papa pretended it was very wicked. I don't know anything else."

"I hope he is good-looking," said Miss Vincent. "I like handsome men. You see, Amelia, I'm nobody, and of no family,

and can do as I please, or rather I *could*
do as I please, if I had plenty of money.
So I should not hesitate for a moment to
fall in love with a handsome man, though
he were only a glazier. But you must
think of the high respectability of your
people. Glass is brittle, my child."

A curious contrast were these two young
women as they conversed together. Jenny
Vincent's monkey-like quickness differed
widely from the rather stolid and sullen
character of Amelia. Jenny was much
amused at the situation. She had not
been long at Mrs. Grimes's Seminary, but
during the time she had seen that the old
lady's notions of discipline were not very
lenient. Her pupils were generally spoilt
children of good family—often the daughters of officers absent in India. They

came to school for the most part with very lofty ideas of their own importance, having been waited upon with great deference all their lives. Mrs. Grimes just reversed the picture. She made these pouting peevish aristocrats do real work. The education was elegant; the fare was perfect; there were pleasant evening entertainments; but if a girl were restive, she was made to scrub a floor, or polish a grate, or clean the shoes of her schoolfellows. It was vain for her to refuse, as a fare of bread and water soon brought her to her senses.

Jenny Vincent explained all this to Amelia in a low whisper, lest perchance they might be overheard. She was anxious to save her young friend from all trouble and humiliation. Amelia was wild with indignation that her father should have treated her in such a way, and vowed she would not stay in the house another moment. Jenny feared she would do something foolish.

"You silly creature!" she said. "Can't you trust in me? I am trying to make things easy for you. If I were to ring the bell a couple of maid-servants would come, and you would be locked up in a dark room all night, to be brought before Mrs. Grimes in the morning. You will be very comfortable here, if you are wise, and you will have me to talk to; if you don't listen to common sense, I shall think you really are in love with that confounded young glazier. Why, you ought to think yourself very lucky to meet me here. If you hadn't, I don't know what might have happened to you."

"I am not afraid," said Amelia, who had both strength and courage. "I think I can take my own part pretty well. I am so disgusted with papa. If he had said he wanted me to go to school I should have been glad enough, for I know I am very ignorant. What am I to do, Jenny?"

"Do what I tell you exactly. If Mrs. Grimes finds a girl indolent or disobedient she punishes her in some way that is sure to make her remember it. But if a girl does her work and gives no trouble, she is thoroughly kind. Now can't you pretend to be better than you are for a time, and conciliate the old lady, who will at once think your father has been treating you badly? I don't see why you should not be twice as happy here as you were at home, except, of course, for that glazier."

"What a little wretch you are!" she said. "Wouldn't you have got some brandy for a man who had fallen off his ladder?"

"Of course I should, if he was young and handsome, which no doubt was the case with your glass-mending hero. But now you must go to bed, child. I have already allowed you to stay chattering longer than I ought. My orders are very strict, and I have broken through them because I like you."

"You are always kind, Jenny," she said.

"Well, I like you, Amelia, because you are such an obstinate little goose. And I think there is more in you than you know yourself. My father, who was a philosopher—do you know what that is?"

"I suppose it means he sold news-papers."

"You little muff! Never mind: he used to say that half the girls of the day would be a deal wiser if they were properly treated. His idea of properly treating me when I was troublesome, which was pretty often, was a touch or two with a slight cane."

"What a shame!" said Amelia indignantly. "I would not own such a father."

"Upon my word," said Jenny Vincent, laughing, "you are too absurd, Amelia. I deserved all I got, for I was a pert little minx, and he was a dear wise old father. Wasn't that better than your father's taking you in a sly way to a school where you may perhaps be treated in the same way, if you give any trouble?"

"What!" said Amelia.   "Dare not say such a thing."

"Don't talk so loud, you tiresome girl. I shall give you up if you won't be good. Now listen to me.   To-morrow you are to treat me with great respect, as if you were dreadfully afraid of me ; and you are to go on doing that, regularly.   You are not to speak to me in the class-rooms without a curtsey.   I want to keep you out of mischief, and if you do all I tell you there will be no difficulty.   Always do exactly what I tell you.   Do you agree ?"

" I do," said Amelia.

"Now go to bed, then ; and remember that in the presence of others I shall speak to you quite harshly, and you must take it quite humbly.   You understand ?"

" I think I do."

So they went to bed, Jenny Vincent hoping that she had made Amelia, for whom she had a strong liking, understand her position; while Amelia herself, cheated as she had been by her father, felt that she was alone in the world except for Jenny. Jenny was soon asleep, but Amelia lay long awake, wondering. She was slow, but it was the slowness of an ungrown undeveloped brain. In fact, this gawky girl had run to height and weight; had been forming body at the expense of brain. A good judge might have divined a statue in the marble, and predicted that she would be a fine woman at forty— before which age a fine woman is almost impossible. Now, with a dim gas-jet burning, she looked round the room with its two white beds, and thought over her position. Her bed had its head towards the front wall of the house, so that the window was close beside it. Jenny was breathing quiet breath, and sleeping a tranquil sleep in the opposite corner of the room, taken diagonally. A very clear conscience had Jenny Vincent, and a splendid digestion; so, when she slept, it was sleep of the right sort. She had no troubles; she was only a governess, even as her father was only a newspaper dealer; but they did their duty in their special grooves. Jenny was not pretty; indeed, she had one of those quaint faces which the majority of folk deem ugly; but, as she lay with her head above her arm on the pillow, and her breast moving slowly to

the music of sleep and the wonder of
dream, I think some spectators would have
said " That's the very little girl for me."
It would be hard upon Amelia to describe
her in this delicate situation, seeing that
she was utterly unformed. To-night she
could not sleep. Her new position worried
her. She hated her father's deceit. She
tossed and turned upon her bed, and
envied Jenny, who was doing a little
musical snore in the contrary corner. I
often think that the human nose (especially
the female human nose) might be educated
into a musical instrument that would beat
the flute out and out. Ladies who can
snore musically may communicate with
the author, who will bring the matter
before the Royal Academy of Music.

This world is full of coincidences. How

often you meet a man who ought to have
been your father, only your mother refused
him! How often the man who ought to
have been your father has a great deal more
landed property than the man who was!
How often you meet the clerical cad you
despise just round the very corner where
you strolled to avoid him! How often an
old schoolfellow whom you had tunded in
your boyhood turns up from Australia,
and suggests that he should like to borrow
five pounds! How often the editor of
some periodical to which you send an
article happens just to have acquired
another on the same subject by a very
high authority! How often the lady whom
you ask to marry has just a few hours
before engaged herself to your dearest
friend or fiercest enemy!

This dissertation is designed to lead to a very curious coincidence, not to be omitted from this truthful narrative ! I hope my readers remember Cis Englehurst's adventure, and how the Slippery One and the Parson came to grief over their attack upon her bedchamber. These two worthies had as yet eluded the police, even with Castelcicala's aid; and Crake thought it was time for them to do something fresh; and he indicated an ostentatious City man, who dressed his wife in most aggressive diamonds. Slippery Jack and the Parson were quite willing; and marked down the place. Unluckily for them, they made a mistake. The stockbroker with the bediamonded wife lived in a row of detached villas, each much like the other. Next door to him was the highly-exclusive seminary of Miss Grimes. Slippery Jack and his friend, the Parson, by ill-luck turned into the garden of the seminary. Their programme was, to enter the stock-broker's room, which was on the second floor front, by means of a rope ladder, to frighten him and his wife into silence and non-resistance by the exhibition of revolvers, and to walk away with the dia-monds. The cleverest men make mistakes.

They got their rope ladder up quietly enough to the window of the room in which Jenny Vincent and Amelia Laing were in bed—I can't say *slept*, for Amelia was sleepless. She was thinking over her position; wondering why her father had been so cruel; trying to think what she should do if Miss Grimes became tyran-nical. Under the pressure of a new trouble this child's slowly-developing brain became more workable, and she thought with clearness hitherto unknown to her. And, while she was thus thinking, little did she know that Slippery Jack, having reached the top of the ladder, and placed against a pane of glass a piece of brown paper smeared with treacle, was noiselessly breaking that pane. It was soon done. Then he opened the window fastening, threw it up, and sprang into the room.

Amelia's nerves were high-strung. She had gone through a troublous day : her thoughts were growing clearer, her courage greater. Moreover, she felt her latent physical power. When the Slippery One entered the room, she jumped out of bed and caught him by the throat. She was a young tigress suddenly aroused to wrath. The

Slippery One's revolver went off as he fell upon the floor, and the bullets impinged on the opposite wall. Jenny Vincent, awoke by the noise, sat up in bed in an amazed state. The Parson had of course decamped when he saw the state of affairs. He was not the man to put his pious person in peril for any friend.

All the inhabitants of the seminary, in various states of undress, were quickly on the spot when those pistol shots were heard. A passing policeman heard the ' noise, saw the light in the window, climbed the rope-ladder, and threw his bull's-eye on a curious tableau—many feminine folk in light attire crowding into a bedroom, where a tall girl in the lightest attire of all held a scoundrel by the throat, with her foot upon his breast. A regular heroine

looked Amelia, who thought of nothing
but the deed she had to do, and did not
consider her airy costume even when the
policeman entered and deftly put the hand-
cuffs on her victim. But when the man
was taken away and the house grew quiet,
she crept into bed and cried a little ; for
the sadness of her life was troubling her,
and she began to think the world was full
of unhappiness and misadventure. Jenny
Vincent heard her sobbing, and came and
tried to comfort her, but she said,

"Go away, Jenny dear. I am better
alone."

She was quite the heroine of the seminary next day, poor child. Mrs. Grimes
had a special supper in her honour, with
actual champagne—a liquid not too frequently seen in ladies' seminaries. The

girls of the establishment, most of them high-tempered young wenches, of hot patrician blood, who had been sent for Mrs. Grimes to reduce them to order in her own way, were all mad about this new-comer, whose first act was to take a burglar in the very act. The seminary had never seen so festive a night; and I fear that even the Misses Grimes, stern as they were, took quite as much champagne as was good for them. It was far on in the short hours when the festival finished. It had been quite a holiday, and these young rebels were all happy. When Amelia and Jenny found themselves alone, Jenny said,

"What a day! And what a night before it! And how brave you are! I shall never fear robbers with you in the room."

"I don't fear anybody much," said

Amelia, who was undressing as rapidly as she could. "But I should like some one to love. Good night, Jenny."

CHAPTER IX.

THE SLIPPERY ONE.

ALOUETTE.—Some one to love, papa. Yes, that's the wish
 I have.
Some one with whom to listen to the nightingales
When they are singing old delicious love stories ;
Some one to watch me as I slumber quietly,
And perhaps disturb my dreams with just a kiss or
 two.
ASTROLOGOS.—Girls are such fools. Some one to plague
 and worry you,
Some one to take advantage of your weaknesses,
Some one to make a silly little slave of you.
       The Comedy of Dreams.

POOR Amelia, heroine of this great
adventure, cared nothing that she
was probably the first school girl who had

ever captured a burglar. She wanted
some one to love. It certainly had been
the want of her life. Her father's selfishness and her mother's weakness left her
without any object or ideal. Perfectly
innocent was the poor girl, or she might
have gone wrong in her desire for some
sort of affection; but, though awkward
and dull, she had the natural instinct of
goodness, and so she merely longed for
consolation. She was quite ready to love
Jenny Vincent very much indeed; but this
malapert Jenny could not help making
occasional fun of her; and fun of that sort
was a thing Amelia did by no means understand. She was a girl with whom friendship meant something—a rare thing among
girls.

I think girls should learn Latin, if only

to read Cicero *De Amicitia*. One of the weak points in modern life is the decay of real friendship. It is perishing among men, and seems to have altogether perished among women. It is a flower of life worth careful culture ; and I rejoice to say that I have a few friends (a very few) who would do for me what I would do for them, even though life were on the risk. And among them are ladies ! A note of ejaculation is needed. Can a lady, thinks the ordinary dolt, be a perfect friend to a man without what your Old Bailey barrister would call " ulterior purposes ? " I trow not. It must be Platonic love, or love warmer than the Platonic. Dear reader, seest thou the result hereof ? It shuts women out from the friendship of men ; shunts them—reduces them to con-

verse with nobody save curates and lady's-
maids. The dull folk in an agricultural
parish, if they see a lady walking with a
gentleman, instantly whisper something
wrong; the parson, if he is a young fool,
brought into the world to disestablish the
Church, picks up this faintly-whispered
gossip; after which that lady's life becomes
a misery to her. Of course her relations
get frightened, and it is always your nearest and dearest who say the falsest things
about you. As the wittiest Canon of St.
Paul's remarked, the most dangerous animal to let loose among women is a wild
curate.

Nobody burgled on that particular night:
still a heroine awoke Amelia next morning.
The girl's brain was growing rapidly. She
thought much of her situation. She began

to think of her father with the careless
contempt which certainly he deserved.
He had got her to school by a stratagem.
She was quite well aware that to be at
school would be of service to her, and she
already, in a new situation, widely different
from that in which she had spent the
greater part of her life, felt her mind ex-
panding. Amelia Laing was a plant of
slow growth, but strong. A wise father
would have made a splendid woman of
her. Laing merely regarded her as a
nuisance, though he saw possibilities in
her; but he did not see how to develop
those possibilities.

She slept, but not dreamlessly, that
night. She was the heroine of the hour.
Even the autocratic Mrs. Grimes, who all
her life had been horrified by the thought

of robbers, flattered this new pupil who had actually caught one. There was, however, a difficulty raised by the Miss Grimeses or the Misses Grimes. I forget which is Lindley Murrayish. Ought a young lady to jump out of bed with nothing on but a night-dress in order to collar a robber? Is it proper? The Miss Grimeses or Misses Grimes, thought Amelia ought to be rewarded for catching that burglar, but punished for doing it in so light a costume. Mrs. Grimes held a different opinion.

"If the girl had waited to dress, my dears," she said, "we should all of us have been murdered in our beds, or something of the kind. I think of giving her a gold watch as a memento of the affray, with an inscription saying she vanquished a robber with a revolver."

Mrs. Grimes's daughters did not often argue with her much. The old lady was a quaint mixture of kindness and severity, and would stand no nonsense. They thought this proposed extravagance of hers a mistake, but they dared not remonstrate, so they said nothing, hoping that she would forget all about it.

Amelia continued the heroine of the hour. Mrs. Grimes was kinder to her than she had ever been known to be to any school-girl. Even the Penthesilean daughters petted her. As to the girls, they were all mad about her; they forced presents upon her, the delicate trifles girls love; they even got up a subscription among them, and bought for her a jewel-studded dagger of Toledo steel, "the ice-brook's temper," which was nominally a

paper-knife. That seminary for young
ladies grew very indolent; even the reso-
lute Mrs. Grimes could not keep order.

And then, think! What a delight!
Gentlemen calling on this important question. "*The Marquis de Castelcicala and Mr.
Cotton.*" All the seminary was alive to see
the Marquis : but I think Amelia was
more on the alert to see that glazier. She
was rather frightened about it, though.
Jenny Vincent had heard her confession;
might she not tell, and get her into
trouble ? Mrs. Grimes, it was well known,
permitted none of her fair pupils to be in
love. Even Amelia, after her heroic
achievement, would be made a martyr if
she were suspected of a flirtation with
anybody — especially a mere working
glazier. She did not, of course, know

how Cotton came to be there; still less
that her father, wickedly astute, had caused
the rumour to be spread that she had gone
away with him. Had she known of that
paternal trick she could not have spoken
to him.

The Marquis, who had come to London
the moment news of the affair reached
him, wanted to ascertain precisely what
had occurred, and whether any clue was
obtainable to the Slippery One's companion
or companions. With him, besides Cotton,
came a sagacious detective, who was supposed to have the keenest scent of all the
Scotland Yard sleuth-hounds. But for
the quick look of his eye you might have
taken Inspector Fox, from his indolent air
and well-made dress, for an unoccupied
fashionable man, who seldom did anything

except dine, play whist, and dance. Indeed, his nickname among his comrades
was the "Lounger," for he managed, by
his *insouciant* air, to evade recognition as a
detective by all but the most experienced
thieves. To Mrs. Grimes and her fair
flock, some members of which he had to
interrogate, he was rather unintelligible,
but they certainly did not connect him
with the police force; and their eyes were
chiefly fixed on the handsome Italian, who
was just the sort of man to fascinate girls.

"I have seen him before," whispered
Jenny Vincent to Amelia. "He used to
buy newspapers at my father's shop. He
is a conspirator."

Amelia shuddered.

"How dreadful!" she exclaimed.

The only conspirators she had heard of

were those who, in *Mangnall's Questions*,
then the gospel of the seminaries, murdered
Caius Julius Cæsar. She thought them
base wretches; but the Marquis did not
look at all like a base wretch. In any
company he would have appeared a man
of distinction. He had an air of easy
command. To these fluttered schoolgirls
in Miss Grimes's dovecote he was as great
a wonder as Apollo to the shepherdess of
Thessaly, what time Admetus was King.

Mr. Fox examined the room which the
Slippery One had entered, and questioned
everyone who had a chance of seeing
whether the Slippery One appeared to
have companions. In this way he got no
information; but, when he came carefully
to inspect the front garden, he traced with
little difficulty the footprints of two per-

sons. The Slippery One had a foot like a lady's, and was wont to wear elegant boots of a light description ; the Parson had a flat splay foot, which Hoby himself could not retrieve from ugliness. It was a good deal like a flat iron. The physiognomy of detectives has much to do with the human foot, a very tell-tale member. Your thief walks not like your honest man. Inspector Fox could find traces of no third foot, so he concluded that the job was attempted by these two men only.

But, not hurrying his investigation, he found something more, which proved eventually to be of great importance. Down in the midst of an aucuba there lay a small book, bound in red morocco, and lettered " Common Prayer." The parson, proud rather of his clerical nick-name, had set up what looked like a Prayer Book, having, indeed, a gold cross on its red cover, and elaborate clasps; but which, really, was a memorandum book. In it he had written ribald songs, which he was fond of singing in the thieves' resorts, having a fine tenor voice and a good ear. Among these songs were various memoranda, all in cypher. The Inspector pocketed that book with great satisfaction. Nobody noticed the find, and he told nobody: a shrewd fellow, he liked to keep his secrets to himself.

When they were gone, after being compelled by Mrs. Grimes to take that abomination in the way of refreshment, sweet cake and sweeter sherry, which caused the courtly Marquis to make a wry face, what a babble and chatter there was in the excited school! All idea of lessons and classes was abandoned. Even the music-master, that most important of all professors in the eyes of the schoolmistress, had to give up his work and take holiday. All the young heads were in a whirl of excitement, and Mrs. Grimes, finding that nothing could be done with them, sent them all out for a walk on Wimbledon Common, and promised them charades and proverbs and a dance, if they chose, in the evening. She was a wise old lady, and knew how to mingle strict discipline with occasional fun. The girls all ran away with delight to put on walking costumes, and were soon trotting briskly across the breezy common towards Richmond Park, where, besides the big trees and the deer, they saw a little gentleman walking in profound meditation, and were quite unaware it was Earl Russell, pondering over a letter to the *Times*. They came back gaily to their afternoon meal, and the day ended with the saturnalia which Mrs. Grimes had promised. One charade was a great success. In the first act there was a parliamentary assembly, with a Miss Grimes as speaker, and a lively debate was carried on as to the expediency of depriving the male sex of all political rights. This ended in a division, when the majority in favour of the proposal was enormous. Jenny Vincent was the soul of this, for her father had described to her the methods of Parliamentary procedure, which he knew well, having himself been a reporter. Scene the second was a young lady dressed as nearly to resemble a page as seminarist decorum would permit: and the terrible way in which that page smashed glass, to the horror of his mistress, was almost beyond what pages ever do. Need I say that in the final scene Jenny Vincent, with a nightdress over her frock, captured a nocturnal burglar of as ferocious aspect as could be found in the place? Amelia was hard pressed to react her own heroism, but firmly declined.

.

CHAPTER X.

INSPECTOR FOX.

Vulpes in antro.

CASTELCICALA and his companions held council; all that the Inspector would say was that he felt certain that the Parson was one of the robbers, and should take steps to arrest him. The fact that the two scoundrels were known comrades, and the footmarks found in the garden, of which Fox had taken careful tracings in the

presence of the Marquis and Cotton, would
have justified an arrest; but having the
blasphemously-lettered memorandum-book
in his hand, Fox felt an absolute certainty.
Anxious to make an inspection of the book,
he parted as early as he could from his
companions, and sat down at home to see
what he could make of it.

Not much, many people would have
thought; it was written in a hand most
villanous, and the private entries were in
several different cryptograms. Fox was
not to be baffled. He sat down in his
own sanctum, filled his pipe with honey-
dew that had been slightly moistened with
whiskey, took a magnifier, and examined
the rascally volume.

Fox's sanctum was a curiosity. He was
a bachelor—wedded to his vocation. To

be a thief-taker is not a very high vocation, but it is an uncommonly useful one. Fox, whose father was a village schoolmaster in Cumberland, with a remarkable capacity for mathematics, was intended to be something of the same kind. But when he was about seventeen, being in the town of Kendal on errands from his father at Milnthorpe School, he saw a curious-looking fellow sneak out of a small house just below the ruined castle wherein the eighth Harry's sixth Queen was born. The manner of the man excited his suspicion; moreover, he wore a great-coat (not at all requisite, as it was one of those hot summer days which never now occur), and it had many pockets, and bulged immensely here and there. He shut the door stealthily. Fox, a mere slip of a boy,

followed the man, who walked toward the
town, at first slowly, then as quickly as he
could move on. Fox did not lose sight of
him. Presently he turned up an alley
between two houses, with an entrance door
on each side of the passage—an arrange-
ment often observable in the Cumbrian
town on the Kent. Fox, noticing that he
slinked round into a courtyard at the
right, looked about for a policeman, and
actually found one! The capture was
made : David Lipsett, the chief constable
of Kendal, was so delighted with the boy's
cleverness that he contrived to persuade
the schoolmaster to give him a chance in
the force. His remarkable acuteness soon
made him a position, and by the time he
was two-and-thirty he was recognised as
almost without an equal. His comrades

were not jealous of him, for he had no
vanity about him. Moreover, from what I
have seen of gentlemen in the detective
profession—and very gentlemanlike fellows
some of them are—they work in unison
remarkably well.

In Fox's sanctum many were the tro-
phies. Here hung a revolver; there that
cruel weapon known as a life-preserver;
there again a set of knuckle-dusters. He
had a beautiful collection of centre-bits,
and jemmies, and false keys enough to
open all the doors in London. Also, he
had a unique library of thieves' diaries; for
there is literature (if not much honour)
among thieves, and a collection of their
contributions to the *belles lettres* would be
a very pretty supplement to the Newgate
Calendar.

His last volume, just obtained, Inspector Fox regarded as the gem of his collection. He pored over it, smoking thoughtfully. There were, as I have said, songs such as the fraternity loved, the typical one of which is :—

> " In the depths of the stone jug I was born,
>> Fake away !"

Some, of course, were too abominable for citation; others, however, rather amusing for their curious adaptation of an inferior poetical faculty to the rascally vocation of thievery. Here is an example:

> " Maidenhead Thicket's a jolly place
>> For us of the Road, a gallant race:
>> There I robbed a Parson once,
>> But I gave him his sermon back, the dunce.

> " Ay, and I robbed a hunting Squire,
>> His scarlet coat all covered with mire;
>> He clubbed his whip, and he made a fuss,
>> But he didn't like my blunderbuss.

" And I robbed a bevy of maids in white,
Who were going out for a merry night,
And one I kissed, a wicked young thing,
And, fool that I was! gave back her ring."

Of this sort of thing there were many
stanzas, which Fox stayed not to read.
And there was a rollicking chorus, running,

" Hounslow Heath is wild and free,
And on Wimbledon Common good fun there'll be ;
But Maidenhead Thicket,
Ay, Maidenhead Thicket,
Is the merriest place for a robberie."

But between songs and careless memoranda came little bits in cypher, which the
Inspector perused with infinite care, feeling sure that they concealed valuable
secrets. Late that night he sat up, smoking, examining, analysing; forgetting his
food, in fact, till it was too late to go anywhere in search of a supper, and he had
to content himself with very meagre fare.

He cared little. By degrees he discovered the partial meaning of many entries, and found a clue to more robberies than one. He was delighted. There was one entry which gave him some trouble; but he worked at it resolutely, for it was dated, and the date was just before the Engle-hurst robbery. Thus it ran—

" Djcpssjz: Smks : Cscni."

This, though it looks mysterious, is one of the easiest of cyphers to an accomplished cryptologist—one, indeed, which no experi-enced cypher writer would use, since the initial letters are so sure a guide to a prac-tised and acute intellect. When the Inspector looked at that first word, a mo-ment of divination came to him; had he remembered any of the Greek his father had vainly tried to get into his head by flagellating another part of his person, he would have echoed the famous exclamation of Archimedes, when he rushed naked from the bath through the streets of Syracuse. Eight letters in that first word; eight letters in the word *Diamonds.* He applied the test. Yes; *Djcpssjz—Diamonds!* Then he tried *Smks . . . . Slip !* of course, the well-known abbreviation of the Slippery One.

Cscni took little time to solve. When he made it out, this grave inspector flung his pipe into the fire, and sprang up and danced what dimly resembled a hornpipe gone mad.

For *Cscni* was the cypher for *Crake*; and Fox saw at once that Spider Crake, who had been suspected yet undetected for years, was the plotter of the great robbery.

He spent no further time in his investigations, but turned out, at about two in the morning, and ran at double quick to Scotland-yard, to see whether Colonel Henderson might perchance be there.

"Old Crake's the real Slippery One," thought Fox, "but we've got him now."

CHAPTER XI.

PERDITA.

"Alas, the life that once we lived has fled away;
 Lost, lost, beyond the hope of a recovery.
 Love's blushing flowers have faded very long ago;
 And if there was a creature strangely beautiful,
 Who caught your heart within her hand and crushed it
    there
 Till the blood left it—who could fool and flatter you
 In the sweet summer, under leaf-tent tremulous,
 With ripe rose-mouth that your sun-kiss made rosier,
 And then who did * * what's nameless * * call her
    Perdita."

Comedy of Dreams.

NO secret lasts for ever. Accident is the great discovery of mysteries. When the Marquis de Castelcicala met the lady known as Perdita in that market-garden at Bedfont, his exclamation was—

"My God! Impossible!"

Well might he thus exclaim. He had last seen her, white as a swan of Thames, in a glorious ball-room, the wonder of the dance, the delight even of her husband, a crotchety young peer with an idea that he was specially born to set the Thames, if not the Atlantic, on fire, and that women were inferior animals. If there had been any man for whom Perdita cared, her manœuvering mother would not have managed that marriage. If she had then known Castelcicala, for instance, even though she might not have fallen in love with him, she certainly would not have accepted Viscount de Rootz. Women do not judge men by their physical stature only, though that necessarily is a strong

element in a man's success with them;
they consider, also, their mental stature,
which they are abler to appraise than
many of us think. The instinct of a
woman guides her very surely in such
things—she can tell a scholar from a
pedant or a poet from a poetaster more
readily than your accomplished critic who
has been trying to do that kind of thing
all his life.

"My God! is it possible?" might have
been Perdita's agonised exclamation when
she found herself married, by sheer
maternal pressure and worry, to this
clever-stupid gorilla-graceful young Viscount, whose father had been an illustri-
ous failure in statesmanship, and who
hoped to eclipse his father by going in for
literature. When he had wedded Perdita,

through her mother's strenuous exertions,
he did not in the least know what to do
with her. The stately creature was far
too good for this excitable shallow-brained
young Viscount. She began married life
with a little aversion, which soon grew to
contempt. Cleverer than average men, he
was so conceited that Perdita would have
preferred the company of a dull fellow.
Having a clear strong brain of her own,
whereof she was serenely conscious, it
worried her horribly to have for a husband
a man of fidgety conceit.

Some time after her marriage, Castelcicala
met the Viscountess, and they became very
good friends. The Marquis admired her.
He was a chastely poetic admirer of many
women, and was wont to write them songs
and sonnets, caring no whit what dull

husbands or sullen brothers might say. He laughed at jealousy, though native of a land where it is much cultivated.

He flirted pleasantly with the Viscountess, while the Viscount was lecturing at the Quebec Institute on " Matrimony in its more Eccentric Developments." He danced with her at Lady Lotos's in Park Lane, while the Viscount was asking the House of Lords for leave to bring in a bill for the Higher Education of Women, and delivering a most eloquent speech, which drove the Lord Chancellor from the Woolsack in search of brandy and soda, and which the reporters cruelly compressed into three lines. He walked with her, on long emerald lawns by the Thames, at a Twickenham garden-party, when the strawberries and the girls were at their freshest—and the chattering world thought that the tall, mobile Marquis, in black velvet and superb point-lace, was a more fitting match to Perdita—all white, from tossing feather to dainty fringe of dress—than the perky-jerky little Viscount, who was at that moment attending a meeting of the Society for the Suppression of Vice, and holding forth eloquently on the importance of suppressing one Rabelais, and also several loose dramas by a person called Shakespeare. They were pleasant social friends, and nothing more—save that the Marquis, being once the friend of a lady, would defend her to the death against any peril. For him chivalry was not dead. He saw this beautiful girl married to a man wholly her inferior ; he held friendly intercourse with her without the least idea of

aught beyond. But "damned good-natured
friends," to use Sheridan's happy phrase,
made all manner of remarks to the Viscount, and he, afraid to speak to Castelcicala, showed a sulky coldness, which the
Marquis easily divined the meaning of.
De Rootz could not understand his wife, and
sullenly resented the fact that another man
could. He made himself as disagreeable
to her as possible, and, as he was never
agreeable in his happiest moments—which
were when he was talking of himself and
of his ideas for reforming the world,—it
may be assumed that poor Perdita had a
trying time of it. The Viscount was not
irascible, nor was he exactly sulky towards
his wife; he nagged. Whatever happened,
she was in the wrong. She struck at last,
and treated the poor little man with a cool

and lofty contempt which maddened him, and which drove him, as the œstrus drives the ox, into fresh eccentricities.

Just then Castelcicala went back to Italy, much to poor Perdita's distress—for in him she had found her only safe adviser. Just then her Viscount determined to go to China, desiring to get up that empire in a month's travel or so, and to dictate a book to a secretary which the artist of his suite should illustrate, and to publish with Longmans or Murray so superb and sagacious a volume that it would give him a high status with both Parliament and the public. That book never appeared. I have observed that some of these young patricians write cleverish books, which befool the ladies, and which are useful to men of letters as a

study of character. One book generally
exhausts them. Living in a social atmosphere over-charged with intellectual elec-
tricity, they catch vague glimpses of the
ideas of other men, and fancy them their
own. The seed germinates; the youngster
grows ambitious; he writes a book; he
seldom writes a second.

"Genius does what it *must*, and talent
does what it *can*," says Lord Lytton, in a
line unforgettable. It might be added that
bumptiousness tries to do what it can't.
That is the vice of these precocious young
peers and baronets who dream that they
were born to reform the world. Porson
once met a gentleman of this sort, who
maintained that no scheme for making
social life perfect had ever been proposed.
"Buy a Greek grammar, sir," said the

curt Professor: "When you have read Plato, I'll talk to you."

Well, off went the Viscount on a wild-goose chase to China, leaving his Viscount-ess to her own devices. She was glad to get rid of him. Of all uncomfortable hus-bands, a young prig is the worst. She enjoyed herself in his absence, and pic-tured him coming back with a pigtail, and setting the fashion of China in St. James's Street. Meanwhile, however, the foolish child was drawn into a very strong flirta-tion with Lord Bellasys. That eccentric and plausible nobleman was always want-ing to elope with somebody. He never fell in love, but he liked an *esclandre*. By what means he induced Perdita to run away with him I cannot imagine, but he did. It was after a ball: he had planned

the thing beforehand, evidently; but Zeus
intervenes now and then, and his lightning
came at the right moment. Perdita often
wondered what could have induced her to
be persuaded to such a step by Bellasys.
The man had an insisting power. He was
burly and pertinacious. He stuck to his
point, and generally got it. That was the
secret of his carrying away the prettiest
peeress in England at that time. But the
God of Storms was too much for him.
The lightning that night killed one of the
horses and stunned a postillion, Bellasys
himself being in a stupefied state. They
dragged on to the nearest public-house,
the Black Dog, and found shelter there.
Bellasys went to bed, after some trivial
refreshment, in a dazed state, in a state
of wonder indeed as to what actually had
happened.

Bellasys went on to town next morning with two horses instead of four, one having been killed by the lightning. He drove straight to St. James's Square. He vaguely wondered all the time what could have happened to Perdita, who had so strangely vanished when he was insensible. Bellasys, like most of us, had just a scrap of human nature about him; and he would have liked to find that Perdita was all right somewhere or other.

So, after a short sleep and a bath, he had his breakfast. Whether life be tragic or comic, one must eat. Over his omelet, Bellasys read his *Times*. Almost the first thing that he noticed was a telegram from Hohan-lai, stating that the Viscount de Rootz, of Great Britain, had been murdered by a set of unintelligible nomads.

When the Foreign Secretary read that paragraph at breakfast, he said,

"Confound those young wandering idiots! Now I shall have a hundred despatches to write."

When Bellasys saw it he said—

"What in the world has become of the Viscountess?"

Ah, our poor Perdita had taken to a calm idyllic life, unaware that she was a widow, forgetful of Bellasys. Peace came upon her in that delicious garden—in the quaint house where Anemone, Ixia, and Hyacinth helped her to tend her blind rescuer. If ever Perdita returns to society it will not be to greet *you*, Lord Bellasys, with any friendliness.

Her disappearance had been a nine days' wonder. The frightened postboys did not know who the lady was, and could not prattle. Her husband was in China, whither I should like to send a good many other young peers and young prigs, not allowing them to return till they could speak and write the language thoroughly. So, after a time, the fact that the Viscountess had vanished was forgotten in Mayfair and was a mere memorandum in Scotland Yard. Then the question of the De Rootz estates came before the Courts. Then the Viscountess was remembered again.

"Pretty sort of girl, wasn't she?" said the Honourable Maudlin Muff, who, if put into petticoats, would have looked a pretty sort of girl himself.

"A very handsome woman, I have heard," said Charles Cholmeley, who had just taken his Double First at Oxford, and was modest for all that.

" A perfect lady," said a gentleman, who, leaning on the marble mantel with one elbow thereon, surveyed the garrulous youngsters with a kindly pity. " If you boys want an excitement try to find her. I want to find her greatly."

This was Mr. Carington.

Time passed, and she was not found. The Viscount's heir-presumptive was a second cousin, and the peerage was extinct. There was no entail. Altogether the affair was so complex that the Court of Chancery deferred all decision, and every possible attempt was made to find the Viscountess.

Perdita meanwhile knew nothing of all this. She lived among flowers and fruits.

She avoided the great conservatories at
the visitors' hours. But, she often thought,
what old acquaintance would remember
the banished Viscountess in the hardworking housekeeper? Picturesque she
certainly looked, and a little like a pretty
masquerader; but the great world in which
she had lived would never dream of her
masquerading in such a way. So she felt
safe, and, in a manner, content. Of Lord
Bellasys she thought with horror and disgust; a shudder passed through her as she
remembered what had passed between
them. It had humiliated her for ever in
her own eyes; had she not obtained this
unusual and unique refuge, she felt that
she must have gone into a nunnery. Of
her husband she thought little. Whether
he was still surveying mankind from China

to Peru she cared not. He had tired her, and to be tired of a person is worse than to hate him, since weariness is a depressing and hate a stimulant feeling. She more-over believed that, wherever he was or whatever doing, he must be better without her, since antagonist natures only irritate each other. He was a clever fretful fidget; she a calm lover of tranquil life. My tame jackdaw, pecking away perpetually at the limbs of an old tree, around which an owl's cage is built, might personify the Viscount, though it is no compliment to wise old Jack; while the owls below, in absolute repose, their great Athenian eyes, with feathered lids, gazing quietly at the scene, would typify Viscountess Perdita.

Castelcicala's advent upset everything. She was perplexed and terrified. Of course

the Marquis, who knew everything that
passed in society, knew that the Court of
Chancery and the heir presumptive
hungered for the missing Viscountess.
So, when he saw her in the blind old
gardener's room, evidently a member of the
family, for the children actually called her
"Mamma," he was taken aback. What
should he do? Perdita recovered herself
almost sooner than he, and told one of the
girls to bring fruit and wine. The fruit
was superb, and the wine, though home-
made, was made most exquisitely.

"Not much better entertainment than
Adam and Eve offered Raphael," said the
gardener. "These home-made wines
cannot vie with the juices of Burgundian
grapes; but here is something that only
England can produce. Fetch the cherry-
brandy, Ixia."

The pretty little girl, standing on tiptoe, opened the glass door of an old-fashioned corner cupboard, full of quaint china cups, glass bottles, silver flagons, and brought therefrom a noble flask of cherry-brandy.

"This," he said, "is my own make, from the choicest Morella cherries of my own growth, bottled down with cognac and noyau, which I import myself, flavoured with the kernels of my own wall-fruit. You will find it the strongest and yet softest cordial made."

After the cherry-brandy had been tested, there was a move. The girls ran away to resume their work. The Marquis and Cotton rose together.

"I must go," said Castelcicala. "Shall you stay and mend more glass, Cotton? You are not wanted yet. When you are, I can send to you."

"Yes," said Cotton, "I will stay if I may."

"O stay, *please!*" said Perdita, emphatically. "It is selfish to keep you, but you have been so kind and useful."

"I will stay," he said.

The Marquis, taking leave of the gardener and Perdita, walked with Cotton out into the garden. When beyond earshot, Castelcicala asked,

"What will the old gentleman do next, Cotton?"

"He generally doses awhile in his armchair at this time in the afternoon."

"Good. I want a quiet talk with the lady. I know her. Is there not a summer-house or some such place where we could have a quarter of an hour's chat?"

Cotton was grown so accustomed to the Marquis that he felt no surprise.

"The still-room is the very place," he said, pointing to a building of pale brick with a chimney of considerable height. It was behind a thick yew hedge, which concealed it from visitors to the garden. "I keep the key. Will you let yourself in, while I go and say you wait for her there?"

"Thou hast an excellent wit," said the Marquis, taking the key. He let himself into a stone-paved room, with a crucible furnace on one side, and a vast still on the other. There was an inner room of the same size, with a wide stone shelf all round it, on which were arranged small stills, alembics, retorts, test tubes, and much other apparatus for botanic chemistry. The gardener had been a great experimenter before he lost his eyesight : but now he could do nothing, and he thought attempting to teach his daughters to aid him would be too hard a task. We need more experimenters in this direction, for there are a myriad vegetals—fruits, flowers, herbs, roots—of whose active qualities we are ignorant. Not a thing does earth produce which has not a definite purpose. I am a teleologist.

No rooms could have been more suited for a private interview; they had been built with sky-lights only, to avoid side-lights when conducting delicate experiments. Only a bird of the air, looking down through the roof-casements, could posssibly carry the matter. Castelcicala rejoiced at this fortunate circumstance.

"O Marquis!" cried Perdita, when she entered, holding out her hands to him, "to think that *you* should have found me, and I did so hope I was lost to everybody for ever. Please tell nobody. Let me stay in peace here, where I am happy—no, not happy, but contented."

"I will keep your secret absolutely, if, after a quiet talk on the subject, you think it right. You are your own mistress, and no one has a right to interfere with your slightest whim and caprice. But now, before I say anything on that question, may I be told how you came here?"

"Have you heard anything shameful against me?"

"Not a word. Who dare say such a a word? All the world knows is that you suddenly and mysteriously disappeared."

"Nothing—now, do tell the truth, dear Marquis—to connect me with Lord Bellasys?"

"Well," replied Castelcicala with a light laugh, " when I came back from Italy, and wondered what had become of you, my friends chaffed me about my anxiety, and said that you had been flirting tremendously with Bellasys. As no doubt they had said exactly the same of you and me, I merely laughed, and remarked that I rather wondered at your taste."

"Ah, so do I. And that is all?"

" Well, I could get no information about you. I did not care to ask direct questions, in case you had chosen to seclude yourself, and wished to avoid discovery, as I find is the case. Of course I heard innumerable rumours—many pure *canards*. A lady of your beauty and rank does not drop out of London life without wild speculations in the papers. One evening, about a month ago, I was supping at White's, when Bellasys came in and spoke to me. Your disappearance was mentioned.

" 'A very strange affair,' I said.

" 'Indeed it is,' he replied. 'I cannot guess what made her leave her home. I fear some sad accident may have happened to her.' "

" The scoundrel!" she exclaimed, and buried her face in her hands, to hide a blush ruddier than any rose ever grown in that garden. "I must tell *you* the truth, Marquis," she went on, raising her flushed face and tear-laden eyes with a stately sorrow. "Tell no one. Bellasys induced me to elope with him." She fell on her knees before Castelcicala, crying, "Am I not the vilest of women?"

He raised her gently.

"Be calm, poor child," he said. "Tell me all you wish to tell."

"I don't know how he did it. I hated him, but he frightened and fascinated me. We drove away after a ball at Lord Ranthorpe's. Passing just here there was a frightful thunderstorm. What happened I don't know, but something dreadful. I was senseless; the good old gardener who brought me in here was struck blind by the lightning. I have lived here ever since, doing my best for him and his daughters."

"London has never heard of that adventure, Viscountess, and never need. Bellasys will not speak, rely upon it. He must have bribed his postillions, or something would have leaked out. Now check your tears and think of real business. Your disappearance has been forgotten. Other romances have filled the newspapers. But your name has again been dragged through the columns of the press, and I fear that one of the penny papers had an article about you the other day quite as delightful as a romance."

" Why this ?" she asked.

" Because a reward of a thousand pounds has been offered for authentic information about you."

"A thousands pounds ! Why ?"

"You see how much people think you worth. Now—don't be shocked—your husband is dead—killed on his travels."

" Poor fellow !" she said—nothing more. It was impossible to grieve for a man who knew not the meaning of love, and who but for weakness would have been a tyrant.

"Yes, poor fellow! He meant well, but well-meaning blockheads do so much harm. Now, my dear Viscountess, calmly think of the situation. Mr. Cyrus de Rootz, of the Foreign Office, will inherit all the Viscount's property unless you re-appear. Your late husband's solicitors are keeping him at arm's length as long as they can, and offering a thousand pounds to find you. Are you prepared, in order to carry out a caprice, to let that prig De Rootz have a fine property which is clearly yours, and with which you could do immense good? Think it over. You have no need to desert the friends you have made here. You might, indeed, find a way of showing gratitude to the gallant old gardener who lost his eyesight in your service. I am by no means sure that a first-class oculist could not restore his eyesight."

" It is a terrible question to decide," she said shuddering.

" One point more let me mention. Bellasys has bribed those postillions to silence; but, if they should guess that you are the lady, that vast reward will send them prying down here, and you will be recognised. For this reason, there should be no loss of time. I propose to go to the late Viscount's solicitors, who are advertising, and to tell them to stop the advertisement, as I know where you are to be found. This really should be done, unless you are prepared to be surrounded by insolent spies and questioned by stupid policemen."

"But, Marquis, will not Lord Bellasys take notice of all this ? Will he not say something horrible about me ? I dread the thought of its being known to the world that ever I was such a degraded idiot as to go away with that plausible villain."

"Leave Bellasys to me. Give me your permission to see the lawyers. Go back to your quiet occupations here, saying no word to anyone, and try to decide what you would wish to do. Don't hurry yourself. I shall tell the lawyers only sufficient to settle Mr. Cyrus de Rootz. Do you agree ?"

"I will do just what you tell me, Marquis," said Perdita. "You are my only friend ; and O dear me, how delightful it is to have a true and trusty friend !"

"I'd be that to any lady who wanted one," he answered; "but to you, my dear Viscountess, I am bound by all the ties of poetic chivalry. In the gay old days we have had our fantastic romance: why should not it brighten again in a future not far away? You were born for a joyous life, and I predict you will have it yet. Good-bye. That boy Cotton remains here. If any unpleasant people come prowling about in reference to that advertisement, leave them to him. I'll give him a hint, without betraying you."

Which he did, as Cotton walked with him to the garden gates.

Castelcicala had no difficulty in getting what country folk call a "lift" back to London. He had deserted his first fair acquaintance, but many more pretty bou-

quet buyers had come down that day. As
the Marquis had not Mr. Hepworth Dixon's
objection to being "smothered with Coun-
tesses" (odd sort of disgust for a man
who once recorded with delight in the
Athenæum the fact that at Kimbolton
Castle the Duke of Manchester actually
handed him his bed-room candlestick!),
he made a merry fifth in a barouche which
contained a Duchess, a Countess, the
Countess's daughter of thirteen, and the
most mischievous and smallest of Maltese
dogs. The Marquis was always welcome
to ladies, being always gay. He never
talked politics (which ladies hate), because
he was a profound politician and a daring
secret diplomatist. He had made women
a careful study, being of opinion that
there was scarcely a woman to be found

from whom a man could not learn something.

When he reached London, after a pleasant drive in delightful commerce with the fair, frank spirits of high-born English ladies he drove as fast as he could to King's Bench Walk. There he saw Mr. Lidstone, senior partner in the firm acting for the late Viscount's estates.

" I come in a hasty way," said Castelcicala, giving the lawyer his card. " I want you to withdraw that advertisement for the discovery of Lady de Rootz. She is alive and well: I have just seen her: she can be produced at any moment."

" Is that so?" said the lawyer, slowly. " Really ! we feared she was dead. You will of course claim the reward?"

" Well," said the Marquis, " you English

have odd notions about money. Take a
reward because I happen to know where a
dear friend is in retirement! I wanted to
save the estate from loss, and to prevent
her from being harassed by spies. Why,
man, if that dear lady wanted twenty
thousand pounds, I'd get it for her in an
hour."

If Castelcicala had not been unmistake-
ably high-bred, the lawyer would have
thought him a swindler. As it was, not
thinking of anything to say, he most
sagaciously said nothing.

"I do not give you the Viscountess's
address," said the Marquis, "because I
have not yet her permission. I hope to
obtain it to-morrow. I met her by accident: she has been living in such retirement as to see no newspapers: she was

unaware of her husband's death. I think she will take my advice, but I thought it well to give her time."

"Very wise, very wise," said the lawyer, shaking a ponderous head, so big that his hatter had to build him hats expressly— formidable structures, in which you might cradle a baby. The hugest heads are not always the wisest."

"Well," said Castelcicala, "I'm glad you think so. Better cancel that advertisement at once, and put Mr. Cyrus Rootz out of his misery by telling him the Viscountess exists."

"I will," said Lidstone. "Thank you very much." He rolled out the words in an unctuous bass that made most people think they meant much more than they actually did.

Castelcicala was resolved if possible to find Bellasys that night. He discovered that he was in town. He spent the whole night in trying to track him, in likely places and unlikely, without success. So, after a short sleep at his hotel, he went to his rooms at the Albany at about eleven, and found him lazily breakfasting.

"Of course you've not breakfasted," said Bellasys. "Join me."

"I seem to have only just supped," said the Marquis, sitting down and accepting some curried lobster from the servant. "Fact is, I was trying to find you all night. I have something quite private to say."

The servant, at his master's signal, left the room.

"Go on, old fellow," said Bellasys.

"Won't lead up to a duel, I hope."

"O, dear, no! I am the only person who knows of your adventure with Lady de Rootz."

"By Jove!" cried Bellasys, dropping his wineglass with a crash, "how the devil did *you* know it?"

"From her ladyship's own lips. I saw her yesterday. The lawyers are looking for her, you know, because Cyrus de Rootz wants to get hold of the estates; they have been offering a reward of a thousand pounds, which I have told them to withdraw."

"I was a confounded fool and knave," said Bellasys, "and she was, and is, I hope, a beautiful woman, a thousand times too good for De Rootz. I have made a fool of myself with women a good many times, but never regretted it so much as this time. What do you want me to do, Castelcicala?"

"Say nothing. If any rumour *should* creep out, and any impertinent fellow should mention it to you, shut him up in your strongest style; horsewhip him, if you like, for daring to slander a lady of the highest character. You owe her reparation."

"I do."

"Then defend her everywhere, if I should induce her to enter society again, should slander touch her. I doubt whether it will."

"Do you think she will speak to me?" asked Bellasys. "You can tell her I really am a reformed character. Don't I look it?"

The Marquis laughed.

"I think you're improveable, my friend. You behave like a trump to my poor little Viscountess, and I shall believe in you."

"I will, by Jove!" said Bellasys.

CHAPTER XII.

BELLASYS.

ASTROLOGOS.—Strong races run to goodness or to wickedness.
The nation that gave Christ gave too Iscariot ;
Isaiah's kinsman cries "Old Clo!" beneath me here;
I wonder what your fate will be, Prince Raphael,
Whose father strongest was of men, and wickedest,
Whose father's father was a King of Chivalry?
RAPHAEL.—Nay, wonder not, old friend : the problem's
soluble ;
I have the perfect power of loving loveliness.
The Comedy of Dreams.

WERE you ever in China, gentle
reader? Hardly probable. If you
desire to go to that marvellous Empire in

imagination, read Chinese Sketches, by Mr. Herbert A. Giles, a member of the Consular Service, a keen observer, and a most delightful writer. I had never heard his name till his book reached me, so I am not giving him a friendly puff—which is better, after all, than the spite which some critics lavish on an enemy, real or imaginary. From that volume I have learnt more of the Chinese than I had ever known before; and, as that great reservoir of humanity, so long dammed up, begins to pour its contents upon the outer world, it is worth while to learn something about the character of the people.

Bellasys has led me to China. Mr. Giles tells a good story of Chinese divination. They hold the belief that if before a new-born child are placed various imple-

ments, the one he chooses as a toy will in-
dicate the bent of his future life.   A
Chinese gentleman who desired his son
and heir to be famous, placed on the table
before him a sword, a bow, a pen.   The
homunculus looked at them with disdain ;
neither war nor letters magnetised him ; he
crawled across the table to a depository of
hairpins and lace and jewels and rings and
other feminine trifles, and found them
vastly amusing. His destiny was manifest.

Had the same experiment been tried on
Spenser Bellasys in his babyhood, I fancy
the result would have been the same.   He
drew no bow—except the long bow, to
ladies.   He had used the sword once—in a
duel for a lady.   He had used the pen
often, in letters to ladies, and in signing
cheques for diamonds and bouquets and a

thousand other things which he lavished without thought on any lady whom he admired. And there were so many.

Now, if Spenser Bellasys had taken the sword as his weapon, he would have made a splendid soldier, fearless and clear-headed. And had he tried the pen, he would, when once he had conquered grammar (a business that always bothered him), have written in a better style than most of us, and put more matter in his work. For Bellasys, though few of his friends knew it, read immensely: there was a most choice library in that bijou Palace in Park Lane, where he often "outwatched the Bear." He knew the English classics well; he learnt history from Shakespeare, like the great Duke of Marlborough; he knew Chaucer well, and the authors before Chaucer, and

could read easily a poem like *The Owl and
the Nightingale*. Bellasys was peculiarly
English; just as Charles James Fox was
English; just as John Bright is English.
There was a romantic element in his
character which it is not easy to find
room for in hardworking decorous London,
where Fashion, Finance, and Hypocrisy are
the ruling trinity. What can Romance do
alongside of these? Fashion spends money
ostentatiously; Finance makes money, to
supply his feminine partner, by methods
which are rather too like swindling; Hypocrisy, dressed in Fashion's latest garb,
goes to a radiant fragrant Ritualist church
on Sunday, sinks on her velvet hassock,
with a sidelong glance at the handsome
curate, in raiment of many colours, who is
intoning, and prays softly for the widows

and orphans that Finance has ruined during the week. How can Romance gain admission to this exclusive society ? He is banished from the Stock Exchange, the ball-room, the confessional ; yet, strange to say, he has a home in the breast of the most eccentric (and, as most folk think, improper) young nobleman of the day.

Yet really there was no harm in Bellasys, as compared with half the people one meets. He was merely *mad*. He was neither a fool nor a coward nor a knave; but a man with irresistible impulses, and not sufficient power of will to check or guide them. When he had done a mad thing he was always remorseful about it; always anxious to make any possible reparation. No man was ever more generous. No man more readily listened to reason from anyone who had the capacity to advise him. Thus he gave way to Castelcicala with perfect readiness, and made promises which he was quite certain to keep.

Yet, when he sat alone that night—or, indeed, early the next morning—in his brilliantly-lighted library—where he had been vainly trying to read, and had tossed book after book on floor or table, for his valet to replace,—he thought over his conversation with the Marquis, and wished he had asked more questions. He pondered over the matter. In that thunderstorm, how had he missed her? Why he found himself at the Black Dog at Bedfont? Could she be anywhere in that neighbourhood? He'd explore, any way.

He rang (it was three in the morning), and said to the man in attendance,

"I shall want to ride at six this morning. Tell Mason to have a horse ready. He will not be wanted to come with me."

Bellasys dozed in his chair before the fire till about five; then he had a cold bath and dressed; then he mounted a chestnut mare that was as fresh as a lark, and rode gaily away to the Black Dog at Bedfont. There had been a white frost: the autumn morning was crisp and clear: he saw a noble sun rise—no novelty to Bellasys. He reached the Black Dog and dismounted, and asked the landlady if she could give him breakfast.

Of course she could. Very soon he had the sort of breakfast he not often ate— bacon, eggs, muffins, tea, a liquid which he detested. But Bellasys was hungry, and did his duty manfully. The landlady, a wizened chattering little widow, served him all the time, for she saw he was no common customer. Presently Bellasys said—

"Is there anything about here worth seeing? I am travelling for amusement, and like to find out anything unusual."

"Well, sir, not much," said the widow. "There *was*, I've heard, the two Peacocks of Bedfont, two old maids turned into peacocks for their sin in being too proud to marry, and a very proper punishment, because 'as proud as a peacock' is a text in Scripture, but they were dead before my time. There's a market garden, where the great ladies come to buy flowers; that's worth looking at, they tell me. I've never any time to go out. The master of it, Mr.

Ringwood, was struck blind by lightning
one night two or three years ago, when he
was saving a lady in a tremendous thunderstorm. I don't know the rights of it;
'twas before my time. They say he married the lady. Another rasher, sir?"

"Thanks, no," said Bellasys. "I will
go and look at Mr. Ringwood's garden."

Asking the way, he walked thither,
wondering all the while whether, by any
strange accident, the Viscountess could be
the lady whom his loquacious hostess had
mentioned. He found the gates. Very
calm lay the wide expanse in the autumn
sunshine. He strolled lazily along, un-
challenged by the men at work, who were
accustomed to allow all strangers to pass
except the obvious tramp. He passed
from garden to garden and flower-house to

flower-house, unwilling to go to the gardener's residence, except it were the last
resource.   He always had faith in his fortune—and this time it did not desert him.
For he pushed open a green door in a wall,
and entered a small square garden, and
there was Perdita—otherwise Margaret
Valence, Viscountess de Rootz—plucking
peaches.   She was alone ; she had an open
basket   on   one   bare   white   arm ;   her
garments were gathered up around her ;
her other arm reached upwards as she stood
on tiptoe plucking the mellow fruit.   This
was a choice walled garden, always locked,
where the finest late peaches were grown.
Perdita liked to pick them   herself, with
delicate care.

Bellasys watched her graceful movement,
unseen, for a while ; then he went forward.

Hearing his step on the gravel she turned round, and greeted him with a stately air of indignant surprise. She said nothing.

"Lady de Rootz," said Bellasys, "I have only just discovered where you were residing, and I come to ask your pardon for my wicked conduct to you. I make no excuses. I want you to forgive me, if you will; and I want to know if there is any way in which I can possibly help you. I heard of you from Castelcicala, who tells me the Viscount's death is known to you. Of course you will now resume your position in society?"

"I don't know," she said, almost fainting. "I think not."

"Let me hold that basket of beautiful peaches," he said, taking it from her white hand, while at the same time he supported her by an arm round her waist. The surprise was too much for her. Her meeting with Castelcicala, and all the news he brought her, had been a trial; but the coming of Bellasys brought a sudden vision of that terrific thunderstorm which had saved her from shame, and punished her rescuer with blindness.

She recovered herself, put aside the encircling arm, and said,

"I forgive you, Lord Bellasys. Now, leave me, please."

"Listen to a few words, Margaret," he said. "Will you be my wife? I loved you madly then: I love you calmly now. I am not the wild fellow I once was." [By-the-way, his reform was hardly a week old.] "I do verily believe, dear love, I could make you happy."

The basket of choice peaches was on the ground, and his strong brown hands grasped her slender white ones, and his great versicoloured eyes, that were blue when he was calm, and brown when he was joyous, and red when he was angry (those eyes were the fascination of the man), looked straight into hers. It seemed as if her soul started out to meet his.

She could not say " No."

She was afraid to say " Yes."

She said nothing.

What she looked I know not, but it was a look that sufficed to make Bellasys take her in his arms, and kiss her lips and eyelids, and say,

" My own love !"

Echo seemed to repeat the simple monosyllables; every corner of the quaint

square garden had the same thing to say.
The very peaches blushed more deliciously
than their wont.

"I am not worthy of you, Margaret,"
whispered Bellasys, "but I will be."

They stood silent awhile, each filled
with a great and difficult thought. Bellasys
spoke first.

"Castelcicala did not tell me you were
here," he said. "A kind of intuition led
me to Bedfont. Now you are found; you
are mine."

"But I am in a strange situation," she
replied. "What would the old blind
gardener do without me, who lost his eyesight for my sake? I have made these
gardens my study: I feel as if returning to
the world would be just as if Eve willingly
left Eden."

"Don't talk sentiment, but sense, my Margaret. If Adam had been an elderly gentleman who lived by selling the produce of Eden, likely enough that Eve would willingly have left it. The present case is clear enough. Let him sell this place, which must be worth a lot of money, and retire, and I'll settle an annuity on him. If he weren't blind, he could take my gardens at the Castle in hand; I haven't been down for four years, and the whole place is in a frightful disorder, and I can get no fruit or game sent up. Shall we go down there, Margaret?"

"I am dazed," she said, holding her slender white hand to her brow; "I ought not to let you persuade me. I ought to hate you. You know I ought, Lord Bellasys. How wickedly you treated me! and then

R 2

you pretended to the Marquis—and to all the rest of the world, I suppose—that you knew nothing about me !"

" What *could* I say without compromising you ? I was thoroughly stunned by that lightning flash. It was some days before I could summon my wandering wits. I was mad enough before, and that adventure made me wilder. I had half an idea of wandering away somewhere, and leaving the world to wonder for a week, and my heirs to fight over my estates for a week of years. You are the only woman I had ever loved—and I had lost you."

He spoke with a strong passion in his face, a strong light in his eyes. Perdita stood before him trembling ; she felt as if she must sink to the ground. She was like a column of water thrown up an Icelandic geyser, which stays clear and pure in the air for a few minutes, as if it were transparent marble, and then collapses suddenly.

" What *am* I to do ?" she cried, in a voice of pain. " O, is there no one to help me and tell me what to do ? O, why am I left alone in the world ?"

" You are not alone," said Bellasys, supporting her tenderly. " Trust me."

" How can I trust you, Spenser Bellasys? Have you not deceived me ? Should I not now be a disgraced outcast if God had not interfered with his lightning ? Why were you not struck blind instead of my good friend who is a father to me ?"

" It would have served me right," he said, in a quiet tone, " if I had been killed that moment. But how if God chose to preserve my worthless life that I might offer you some imperfect atonement ? You don't quite hate me, though you think you ought; and I am ready to do anything within the powers of man to make you happy. Come, dear lady, forgive me. I only want *you*, to be different from aught that I have ever been. All the devils that are apt to dwell in me are cast out by your presence. Don't hesitate ; you have kissed me ; the world is changed for both of us. This is the supreme instant. You cannot go back, Margaret——. You cannot."

She could not. She let him take her in those giant arms of his, and burst into tears.

Half an hour later Bellasys the impetuous was talking to the gardener alone. He had told the old gentleman his story. The gardener pondered awhile.

"I can't see you, Lord Bellasys," he said, "but I like your voice. I do not like your story. Do you mean to be true to this lady, or is it only another caprice of hot blood made hotter by gold without limit? I know you young bloods; you think the world's your foot-ball, to be kicked where you will. You all find that in the long run the world is stronger than the strongest of you. Hercules and Samson were both beaten by women."

"I am very resolved to go straight, Mr. Ringwood—simply and singly for the sake of Perdita, as you call her—who is Perdita no longer, and who will soon resume her place in London society."

"If she can trust you, what can I say?" said the gardener.

"Trust me also. Let me talk of your

own affairs. You will scarcely he able to manage this place without Perdita."

"Not so well, perhaps. No matter. The girls will miss her sorely."

"Why not give up? This place would sell for a fine sum of money. I'll get you an honest lawyer to carry it out. Then come down to Bellasys Castle in North Devon. I can put you into a capital house; there are splendid gardens all in ruin because I haven't been there for four years, and it will be an amusement for you and Margaret to get them into order. The change will do your three little girls good. What do you say?"

"If you like to send me that honest lawyer you talk about, I'll see. This place is my freehold, and I have refused large offers for it, to build upon."

"The goodwill of your business should be worth a large sum,'" said Bellasys.

"It is," he said. "I should like to make as much as I can for the sake of the girls. Go find that honest lawyer. If you do, I shall believe in growing a blue dahlia, or getting cucumbers on the first of February."

As they were talking, the Marquis and Cotton arrived. Cotton was wanted at Englehurst, and the Marquis had come to fetch him.

"You here!" said Castelcicala to Bellasys.

"It seems so. Have you a minute to spare? Come into the garden."

They went out together.

"Look here, Marquis," said Bellasys, "Margaret is going to marry me. How can we manage to account for her absence ?"

"I expected this, but hardly to-day," replied Castelcicala. "Caprice, thy name is woman."

"Don't chaff," said Bellasys. "I'm devilish serious. You were always a good one at devices."

"Well, she's been abroad, of course. Beyond the reach of newspapers. Say Greece. She has been exploring Athens, and all that sort of thing. I'll get a paragraph in the *Morning Post* to-morrow to say that the Viscountess de Rootz, after a long tour in Greece, the Archipelago, and the Troad, is expected soon to be in England. Hadn't I better add that a marriage is rumoured between this beautiful and accomplished peeress and a certain noble lord, who has hitherto shown no inclination to settle down into the happy state of matrimony?"

"Hang it! do be serious. How are you to make it look as if she came from the Continent?"

"Easy enough. She might run over to Calais in a yacht, and come back by the *Castalia*. But there seems no reason for taking that trouble. She may drive, with luggage and in a travelling costume, up to some London hotel, at which rooms can be engaged for her in advance. That can be managed, so soon as she is ready to leave this."

"The sooner the better," said Bellasys, and went off in search of her.

The result of this colloquy was that in about a week a lady, evidently fresh from travel, arrived at Claridge's. She had no attendant but a courier; her lady's-maid, the courier explained, had been left behind —taken ill on the way—your maids Anglaises get spleen when they travel. That courier talked a jargon of many languages. The waiters all laughed at his gibberish.

When Perdita was snug in her rooms, the courier took leave.

"Miladi let Giuseppe savoir if elle a need de lui. Ici la carte, Ladyship."

He presented his card, and went chattering in a mixture of tongues downstairs.

"It is the Lady de Roosh," he said to the head waiter. "Vous voyez, on the tronks. Elle a mooch money. Elle me payez . . . . . . Ah! Voici!" and the voluble courier took from his pockets a huge handful of sovereigns. "Ah, you are good boy, bon garçon. Nous avons de Clicquot together. Come, venez. Six sous avec, sans souçi."

And the courier and the head waiter went off to the latter's den, where they had Clicquot and anchovy toast, and the courier told his companion a long and most interesting story of the Viscountess's travels in Greece and elsewhere, which that waiter forthwith talked about to everybody.

Now, that courier was the Marquis de Castelcicala; yet had he coolness enough to call at Claridge's next morning in his own ordinary costume, and ask for the Viscountess de Rootz. He was shown to her apartment by the head waiter whom he had mystified, and who did not suspect him in the least.

"I am so glad to see you, Marquis," she said.

"And I you, looking so well after your long travels. Just read this, but say nothing. Walls have ears, you know."

On a sheet of paper the Marquis had narrated his conversation with the waiter, stating the adventures he had ascribed to her. She laughed heartily.

" How clever of you !" she said.

" It was very amusing. Keep that as a reminder of where you are supposed to have been. You will have to launch into the ocean of fiction now and then, for vraisemblance' sake."

" Well, I suppose so," she said. " I cannot say I am tired of the world, though I was tolerably content in the Bedfont garden. It was a dull, slow life. I used often to compare myself to a large tortoise we had, that would never stir a yard from the strawberries in summer, or from the hothouse flue in winter. They said he was a hundred years old. I'm sure I felt a hundred years old in those days. I am younger already, now that there seems to be some chance of life."

"You seemed pretty gay at Bedfont," said the Marquis.

" I tried to be gay. It was my duty to cheer the man who had been struck blind for my sake. I was at least thankful. Picture yourself a girl married against her wish to a prig, a pedant, a tyrant. If I had fallen down and worshipped him in a hypocritical way, as his flatterers and parasites did, I might have done with him whatever I pleased. But I saw through him, and he knew it, and was not at all pleased. So, being a creature of impulse,

I suddenly gave way to temptation, from which I was rescued as if by a miracle. Often I compare it in my mind to Paul's vision of Christ in the clouds of Heaven."

"And you will amuse yourself when you are Lady Bellasys?" he said.

"Ah, when I am Lady Bellasys! I have promised: I must do it. But, Marquis, I dread what may come of it."

"There are two ways of looking at the matter," said the Marquis, "one romantic, and the other commonplace. As to the first, Bellasys loves you, that's certain—and you must care a trifle for him, or you would never have listened to him. I consider him to be a man whom the love of a good woman would keep straight; his impulses are stronger than his will, and you must act as his will."

"Tame a tiger, in fact," she said, laughing.

"Yes," he said, "it is very much that sort of thing, but you have a good precedent in Una and the Lion. Ah! a queer coincidence! Your tiger's name is Spenser."

She laughed merrily.

"Now for your commonplace view of the difficulty," she said.

"It is just this. You are supposed to have been travelling. We have done our best to make this supposition plausible. But . . . what three know, the world knows, according to an old proverb; and it is almost certain that some day or other gossip will find a clue to the actual facts. Doubtless they will be misrepresented: but when you are Lady Bellasys scandal will not reach your ears, unless your parson happens to be a Rugby man. People who come anywhere near the truth—especially those who know that dull fellow De Rootz, will say your girl romance has ended as it ought."

"Fancy your calling him a *dull fellow!* That is exactly what he thought he wasn't."

"I know it; but by dulness I mean ignorance of what you are fit for. A good ploughman or blacksmith is not a dull fellow because he cannot understand a *Times* leader or Browning's *Inn Album*, or the parson's sermon all cribbed from commentators. He can do what they cannot. Would you call Delane or Browning or the youthful curate dull, because neither of them can hold a plough or make a horseshoe? De Rootz, I take it, would have made a clever shopwalker at Shoolbred's. It was not his fault that the irony of fate made him a Viscount; but he was not obliged to write silly books and make silly speeches."

"How severe you are!" said the Viscountess.

"I hate fools," he replied.

"Can your ladyship receive Mr. Cyrus de Rootz, of the Foreign Office?" asked a waiter entering.

"By all means," she replied, laughing. "How *à propos!*"

There could not, at the very first sight, be any doubt as to classing Mr. Cyrus de Rootz among those whom the Marquis declared he hated. He might have sat for Thackeray's cabinet picture :—

" Winter and summer, night and morn,
    I languish at this table dark :
My office window has a corn-
    er looks into St. James' Park.
I hear the Foot Guards' bugle horn,
    Their tramp upon parade I mark ;
I am a gentleman forlorn,
    I am a Foreign Office clerk."

Mr. Cyrus de Rooz, though a gentleman forlorn, when working (or lounging) for his country in that magnificent palace over which Lord Derby presides, was a wonderful butterfly of fashion when riding in the Row or flirting with Miss Veriphast at a Twickenham garden-party. Poole dressed him; Hancock found diamonds for his jewelled white fingers ; Hoby fitted his small feet to perfection; Truefitt curled his hair in the most charming style ; Quartermaine found him the prettiest brown mare in London. How did he do it ? There were a few people who knew—and to their cost. He was, though a dull fellow in most things, a better whist-player than either Clay or Cavendish.

When he saw in the *Morning Post* that the Viscountess de Rootz, who had strangely disappeared, had just returned from foreign travel, and was at Claridge's, he would have torn his hair, only he adored every curl of it. His friends at the Foreign Office chaffed him a good deal that morning. He had quite made up his mind that the Viscountess had come to some untimely end; then, as heir to the estates, he might hope to get the title revived in his favour. What should he do? How if he were to marry the Viscountess? She could not be insensible to his faultless style. He determined to call upon her.

Castelcicala took leave as he entered, and Mr. de Rootz looked at him with dismay, as perchance a rival. Well as he dressed, he could not help seeing that a man like the Marquis was likely to efface him.

He talked the *argot* of London society to the Viscountess. He assumed that, while away from England, she had heard nothing of what he thought the only society in which to live. So he delivered himself like a mere scandalous newsmonger of anecdotes of the misdeeds of various celebrities. She was half bored and half amused. Presently he asked her questions about her travels : but she had no need to recall the Marquis's notes, for he did not give her time to answer. He was one of those shallow men, centred in himself, who cannot listen. An infinite conceit made him fancy that he had interested her merely because she concealed her *ennui* and was courteous. Would it be wise to hint anything? he asked himself—to make her understand that he would condescend to take possession of her and her estates, and manage both in his own highly superior manner? What he might have decided we know not, for at that moment a servant announced—

"Lord Bellasys."

On the entrance of that giant of the peerage Mr. Cyrus de Rootz departed.

CHAPTER XIII.

" London's loud sound is echoed in far villages,
  Bringing strange thoughts to people unintelligent."

IT will probably not have been entirely forgotten that Charles Cotton posted a letter from Amelia to Jenny Vincent on the day when he was attending to the glass in Mr. Laing's conservatory. That letter had a curious fate. Little Jenny, like most of her class, was a bird of passage. Among the unfortunate products of our modern civilisation, I take it that few are less satisfactory than the middle-class governess. She is usually but half educated, and almost always ill-mannered. Whether in a family or a school, she is commonly expected to do work almost menial. The middle-class usher is gradually rising beyond the degradations to which he used to be subject—when, as in Goldsmith's time, he was expected to comb the boys' hair, and to sleep three in a bed! Mr. Justice Maule, who might have been the greatest mathematician of our time, had he not been incomparably the greatest judge, was in youth a tutor in the family of a Quakeress, and has recorded his astonishment on the first morning when the smallest of his pupils came to him and said,

"Friend Maule, wilt thee button my breeches?"

But the new movements in education are gradually abolishing all this, and I hope the governesses of the present day are gradually attaining a much higher position. Our forefathers, when they established public schools, intended them for boys and girls also; but the girls have lost their share in those great endowments. For example, while Christ's Hospital educates fifteen hundred boys, many of whom have attained the highest University honours (it should never be forgotten that one of England's greatest poets, Coleridge, and England's most delightful essayist, Charles Lamb, were educated there), it brings up, I believe, less than a hundred girls, and they are trained to be maid-servants and the like! Why is this? It is to be feared that the vast amounts

which are held in trust by the London
Companies for educative purposes are by
no means wisely applied; and this is a
serious matter when the people have grown
alive to the truth of Brougham's apoph-
thegm, "Education renders men easy to
lead, but difficult to drive; easy to govern,
but impossible to enslave."

Jenny Vincent was cleverer than most
of the middle-class governesses, having
had an uncommonly clever father. She
had caught up a smattering of almost
everything, and could lecture girls learned-
ly on Darwin's development, Tyndall's
light, Max Müller's Sanskrit, Gladstone's
Homer, and all the other foam of efferves-
cent brains which comes to the surface of
society. She knew a little of everything.
In her merry father's news shop she had

glanced at all the fleeting ephemeral literature of the time, from the *Quarterly Review*
to the *Echo*, and having the power of reading with rapid ease, and a most retentive
memory, she had really almost as much
miscellaneous information as George Au-
gustus Sala himself, whose reminiscent
faculty reminds one of the net which
brought together the miraculous draught
of fishes. All was fish that came to Jenny
Vincent's net. She read *Tom Jones*; she
also had read a translation of the *Koran*.
She mastered (or mistressed, shall we say?)
four books of *Euclid*, but that frightful
fifth was too much for her. She read the
Arabian Nights, and all Disraeli's and Bul-
wer's novels, and a vast mass of French
literature, prose and verse, which few girls
encounter. Her father, you see, was a

second-hand bookseller, as well as a news-monger, and she, like the Premier, was cradled in a library. Her miscellaneous acquisitions did her no harm; she was as pure and kind a little creature as ever lived.

Now, when Amelia wrote her that un-lucky letter which Charles Cotton posted, she had just left her situation at that address. The school was a stupid one, managed by people who only cared for money; and Jenny, hearing of a pleasanter, or at least a more interesting career under Mrs. Grimes, had gone away. Mrs. Grimes went in for taming wild girls, though she did not so put it in her elegant prospectus, the language of which was as abracadabrian and sesquipedalian as the famous *Times'* review of Thackeray's *Kickleburys on the*

Rhine, which produced his delicious essay on *Thunder and Small Beer*. Thackeray had the finest point on that Toledo rapier of his, and the easiest movement of his wrist, and he went forward to meet the giant of Printing-house Square, and vanquished him. The young gods always vanquish the old giants.

Jenny was to Mrs. Grimes an invaluable assistant, and soon became the leading spirit of this odd acadamy, which was a kind of menagerie of troublesome girls, some tigresses, some monkeys, some parrots, &c., &c. Mrs. Grimes made a *confidante* of Jenny in a short time, for she found it hard to manage her daughters, who wanted to get the authority out of her hands. Jenny became Prime Minister. Susanna and Jemima Grimes soon discovered that Jenny Vincent meant to rule the school, and to manage it by a different method ; it was vain for them to struggle, for the old lady, whose will was inflexible, and who saw that her daughters wanted to carry things with a high hand, welcomed this clever ally, who understood the situation without a word said. Jenny Vincent made Susanna and Jemima angry beyond endurance. If there were any point on which she differed from them, she would coolly say,

"Mrs. Grimes has ordered me to do such a thing."

The old lady, finding herself with such a zealous and intelligent ally, always endorsed what Jenny had said ; and the result was that the school, which would have come to utter grief if Susanna and

Jemima had been left to manage it, went
on admirably. Mrs. Grimes and Jenny
tacitly understood each other. The two
girls—fine women in their way, but without much intellect—were disgusted. Jenny
became the leading spirit of that seminary
for young ladies.

But the consequence of Miss Vincent's
rapid transition from one school to another
was that she missed that letter posted by
Charles Cotton, and it was in due time
returned to Scudamore Lodge by the
Dead Letter Office. By this time Mrs.
Laing, who simply worshipped her scamp
of a husband, and believed his every lie,
had become reconciled to her daughter's
flight, as she imagined it to be.

"The wicked girl," she thought, "to
run away from so good a father!—and

with a plumber or carpenter, or something! I hope she'll be very miserable."

Mr. Laing got this letter of Amelia's back from the Post Office, and did not at all like it. It showed most clearly that his daughter had found him out. A man of his class shudders at the thought of breaking that famous Eleventh Commandment, "Thou shalt not be found out." Besides, even the cruelest scamp may have a little fatherly love—and, when his innocent daughter finds him out, it is not unlikely that he may feel the blow heavily. Strange to say, Mr. Laing did feel this blow more heavily than any he had yet received. He was a successful rascal, quite aware of his own highly respectable rascality. He had always been marvellously callous. He had deceived his wife and the

neighbours all through this business, want-
ing to get Amelia away, and to make it
appear she had gone away with Cotton.
It was one of those combinations which
occur to men who are too astute, or, as
the proverb says, "too clever by half."
Now, when this letter of hers came back
to Scudamore Lodge, and he read his
daughter's simple statement of her troubles
to her old governess, very badly spelt, he
felt a slight pang of remorse. The man
had no heart probably, but he doubtless
had a liver to do duty instead. He began
—hard as it may be to believe—to be
rather sorry for having sent the child to a
school where (as he imagined) all manner
of torture was applied to refractory girls.
Little did he know that she had met her
only friend there, and that her friend had

power to make school work pleasure instead of pain. He resolved to go and see his daughter, and bring her home again; but it was necessary for him to invent some story whereby to account for the whole affair to his wife, and that taxed his imagination.

He was saved the trouble. That night his wife died suddenly of unsuspected heart disease. Strange to say, it drove him almost mad, this sudden death of his wife. He had always somewhat despised her; had inwardly laughed at her blind idolatry of him; had been disgusted at her incapacity for thinking as fast as he thought. Now she was dead: out of Laing's life there was gone his only friend. The phrase is strong, but true. He had no friends. He had plenty of acquaintances, mixed in good society, was popular at

T 2

clubs and the like; yet was there no man to give him the steadfast hand-grip which means, *My friend.*

And why? Because himself he was incapable of friendship. Some men have that inborn incapacity; good fellows, even, who are very pleasant as acquaintances. Laing had never made a friend, except his wife, who was his worshipper. Now she was gone, and he felt lonely in the world; and he thought what a fool he had been to ill-treat Amelia. What should he do? His natural selfishness made him forget his wife, and think about his daughter. Of course she must come home at once to her mother's funeral. He would be kind to her, and try to make her useful for a time. But (looking in the glass and perceiving that his favourite cosmetic left no grey hair apparent) why should he not marry again? There was Miss Cecilia Englehurst for instance!

Coincidences *will* occur in real life as well as in fiction. Amelia was summoned home, and Jenny Vincent travelled with her. Jenny always now had her own way at the seminary, and, liking Amelia very much, she resolved to carry her home. Before she left she said to Miss Susanna and Miss Jemima:

"I hope you will carry on everything as your Mamma wishes, in her orders to me. Here is a paper of instructions."

The two Penthesileas agreed that she was an impertinent little wretch, but obeyed her orders all the same.

Now for my coincidence. Jenny and her charge got into a first-class carriage at

Paddington early in the afternoon. Poor
Amelia was very miserable about her mother's death, though Mrs. Laing had not
been the kindest or wisest of mothers.
When a foolish woman worships a scamp-
ish husband, the result is not likely to be
satisfactory. However Amelia, slow of
growth both in mind and body, could not see
wherein her father and mother were wrong,
and mayhap it was all the better for her.
Amelia was the sort of girl in her teens
who could not be well understood till she
was thirty at least. She could not spell,
or write straight, or keep a correct account, whereas her little ugly friend Jenny
could do these and a thousand other things.
She had not made up her mind upon anything, and Jenny had long since made up
her mind upon everything from the Book

of Genesis to the 365 ways (with one more
for Leap Year) which the French have of
cooking an egg. But we are at Paddington : and the train is about to start. Into
Amelia and Jenny's carriage two gentlemen are hastily admitted. One is, as ‚that
slangy Jenny Vincent thought to herself
(for the high-polite of the governess had
not destroyed the slang of the news-shop),
no end of a swell. It is our friend the
Marquis. And the other is Charles Cotton,
whom the Marquis means to rehabilitate,
now that Crake's rascality has been traced.
I am anticipating the discoveries of Inspector Fox ; but, with that cypher, the
scoundrel must surely be unearthed.

Amelia recognised Cotton, who, for his
part, was a trifle uncertain what he ought
to do. There is social difficulty for a man

who, born a gentleman, is obliged to be a
tradesman ; and it is a difficulty most felt
by those who are really of the noblest type.
When I use the phrase " born a gentleman," I do not mean that he necessarily is
born in a gentlemanly condition of life.   I
mean that he is of good sterling English
blood.   All the true English are gentlemen.

The Marquis, an acute physiognomist,
saw there was something between Cotton
and the rather gawky girl opposite him, a
girl provocative of possibilities, concerning
whom you wonder whether she will be
hideous as Medusa, or supremely beautiful
as Aphrodite.   It all depends on wise
training with girls of slow growth.   They
grow into surpassing flowers, in an atmosphere of love and wisdom, like the plants

in a well-managed conservatory. However, Castelcicala also caught the eye of little Jenny Vincent, and he said unto himself:

"Now, what *is* that girl? She's not an English lady, clearly. The other *might* be, but a rather stupid one. Not lady's-maid —governess, perhaps. I'll talk to her."

Jenny was nothing loth. She would chat with anybody. She had a touch of wit, and was quite free from conceit, and had only just discovered her governing faculty—which was a well-balanced mixture of tact and pluck.

Of course the conversation began with the weather: Providence has kindly made it changeable, to prevent English people from subsiding into eternal silence for want of a subject wherewith to commence conversation. It was, strange fact! a fine day. The Marquis opened on this subject, and remarked that it was always fine weather in Italy, and improvised a quotation in octave rhyme from *Beppo*, for which I have searched in vain. Perchance 'twas in the first edition.

> " Lo, saffron sunset and a sapphire sea!
>> This is not foggy England. Here the climate
> Makes poetry, and pours it into me—
>> And poetry's a thing I waste my time at.
> And here from Sabbatarians we are free,
>> The Virgin's goddess, and the Pope's the Primate,
> Britannic scoundrels make me very sick,
> I almost think of turning Catholic."

"I don't exactly remember that stanza in Bryon," said Jenny Vincent. "Papa let me read Byron. He said there was not a word of harm in him."

"One of the best and wisest men I ever knew," said the Marquis, "solaced his

Sunday afternoons with *Don Juan*. Sunday afternoon in England has become a period of penance. I don't hate Sunday myself, like a character in Mr. Disraeli's last novel; but it really makes me a little melancholy to see the terrific depression which it brings on the people generally. All sorts of miseries are connected with it. The Church of Rome permits amusement on Sunday, after mass; the Church of England used to do the same, but has foolishly contracted the Puritan contagion."

" Would you let the villagers play cricket on Sunday afternoon ?" asked Cotton.

" Would I not? If I were the parson of the parish I would go and play with them, and supply them with a fair allowance of wholesome home-brewed ale. Your clergy —I have watched them long—make an

amusing double mistake. They want to
rival Rome in ceremony and the people you
call Methodists in rigidness. The two
things cannot be reconciled. I say, if
Sunday is rightly regarded, give the people
the noblest morning service imaginable,
with music and colour and incense—and
eloquence if you can get it—and then let
them enjoy what pastimes please them in
the green fields and shady woods. Why
should all you English—men, women, and
children—pass one-seventh of your time as
uncomfortably as if you were sitting in the
village stocks ?"

Jenny Vincent was listening with intelligent amusement; Amelia Laing with unintelligent amazement. Jenny had seen
brilliant men of letters at her father's shop.
The most popular poet of the day had been

there in her girlhood, with holes in his
coat elbows, and looked vainly in the
Athenæum for a review. The greatest
modern humourist had lazily seated himself on the counter and sketched carica-
tures for her amusement. The most
profound of our philosophers had talked
unintelligibly through his nose concerning
the Categories of Kant. So Jenny had a
kind of abnormal education. She was
able to understand unusual people, who
are a perfect puzzle to the ordinary young
lady. Vincent's news-shop had been a
kind of chapel-of-ease to the great Church
of Letters; and Jenny, having met with
some much more curious folk than the
Marquis, was not at all surprised at him.
Besides, she quite agreed with him, often
having felt as if she were sitting in the

stocks as she sat in restless but resolved quietude while an earnest parson poured his platitudes like a shower-bath on his unresisting congregation. Why preach sermons when you have nothing fresh to say? Why not read the Homilies?

They in due time, after a good deal of pleasant converse, reached Englehurst station. Mr. Laing had driven over to meet his daughter, but by accident of a delayed letter the Squire had not heard of the Marquis's return. It was a delicious October afternoon: the wild cherry had turned scarlet among the yellow beech woods; only the oak and ash were stead-fast to their green. So Castelcicala de-cided to walk, and away they strode up the village gaily enough; and the village, which had held that Cotton must have done something dreadful, was entirely in his favour when he returned in such good company. Your villager, especially in the South and West of England, decides entirely on the quality of a neighbour by the company he keeps. If a man has not time to exchange morning calls with county people, or if he cannot stand the annoyance of their sadly insipid conversation, they quarrel with him, and will talk scandal about him horribly, and go so far as to say that he poisoned his washerwoman to avoid paying her bill. Luckily Lord Lieutenants, Deputy Lieutenants, High Sheriffs, and other dignitaries of the sort, were made for calling purposes; so, gentle reader, if you take a house in a country place, and don't want to be taboo'd as a pariah, hire your dignitary! A good dinner will do it, especially if you bring from town a friend from White's or Brooks's who dwells within the pale of excluisve society, and who will, like Theodore Hook, know a man in the country whom he couldn't possibly know in London. After that you are safe. The County recognises you at the recommendation of a Chief Magnate, and you will be at once free to all dinner-parties, balls, garden-parties, that the minor magnates give. I don't envy you, *mon ami*. Those pleasures pall. I would rather, like Charles Fox, sit with my back to a haystack on a summer afternoon, reading the *Prometheus Bound* of Æschylus, and watching the blackbirds cat my cherries.

Of the two parties of travellers I think I must deal first with those who went to

Scudamore Lodge. Mr. Laing gushed over his daughter. He was atrociously effusive to her, and frightfully polite to little Jenny Vincent. That young lady was not easily deluded. When they reached the lodge, there was a tragic scene over the coffin of the poor woman whom Laing had treated as a mere slave. Jenny was sickened by the man's hypocrisy, and wondered much how an honest stupid girl like Amelia could have such a thorough humbug of a father. Amelia was very miserable, of course; but Jenny administered the best consolation she could, thinking all the while that it was a fortunate thing Mrs. Laing had " shuffled off her mortal coil."

I leave for the present the rather uninteresting household at Scudamore Lodge, where Jenny Vincent felt very much like a fish out of water, and go on with the Marquis and the glazier to Englehurst. For Castelcicala, having now an absolute certainty of Charles Cotton's innocence, a proveable certainty I should say, since he had never doubted it, had telegraphed to the Squire for permission to bring him there, and had received that permission at once. Of this Cotton knew nothing. They walked up the village ordering the luggage to be sent on. They passed the Five Horseshoes. The bloated Jenkins sat half asleep, his normal state, upon the alehouse bench, which he had purchased from a late parson of the parish, the Reverend Uriah Urgent, when the church was re-pewed. There he sat, like a turtle on his hind legs; there also Chyle; there one or two more bucolic louts who, drinking his sour-salted beer, poaching and stealing, managed to live without much definite work. When they saw the Marquis and Cotton walking up the village they were a little taken aback. They had hoped that Cotton's disappearance had been final. Of course they had just sufficient sense to know that the Marquis, an intimate friend of the Squire, was an individual beyond their comprehension. Had you asked Bates where Italy was, or what a Marquis was, he would have broken down in his examination. A good many wiser people than he are unaware that Italia is merely the modern form of Latium, and that when Macaulay, in his "Lays of Ancient Rome," wrote of a quarrel between the Latins and the Romans, he was writing nonsense. A good many wiser people than he do not know that a Marquis was the warden of the marches or border lands. Indeed the palpable blunders committed in the leaders of London papers are so absurd that we can forgive the country chuckle-head for thinking that Garibaldi will raise his wages and reduce his hours of working.

The Marquis and his companion reached Englehurst. The Squire received them with his usual generous feeling, which he made stronger in the case of Charles Cotton. For he felt that Cotton had been hardly treated, being accused of complicity in a crime wherewith he had no connexion. The Squire was a man to make ample atonement. It may be worth while here to remark that the men who, having erred in some way, however slight, decline to make apology, do an immense amount of harm. The first impulse of a true gentleman who has made a mistake is to say—

" I am sorry for it."

The man whose vanity (for it is not pride) will not allow him to do this, is a mere cad, and no fit associate for gentlemen. We are all capable of error; surely the right thing, if by any error you have annoyed another person, is at once to admit that error.

The Squire received Charles Cotton in the happy humorous manner which pertains to the old English gentleman, and to him only. This workman in glass felt at home at once; but he was bewildered by the piquant beauty of Cecilia Englehurst when she came forward to greet him. She did it with no manner of patronage.

The Englehursts were human all through, and did not regard other English folk as to be trodden down carelessly. Happily there are many such country squires—else the race of squires would soon perish.

Charles Cotton was a little perplexed at first as to how he should behave in this aristocratic society. It was an unknown atmosphere. He, the hero of that famous pane of glass, the man suspected of being an ally of burglars, was to dine and sleep at Englehurst! He was to have the unimaginable delight of one evening at least in companionship with the lady whom he thought the loveliest in the world—the beautiful Cecilia. It seemed almost too much for him. Never had he gone through any such experience—never before, indeed, been lifted into the Olympian air of the aristocracy. He was in a most excited state. But the quietude of the Squire, the easy grace of the Marquis, the unconscious loveliness of Miss Englehurst, brought the boy to his senses.

CHAPTER XIV.

CLOSE TO THE BEAUTY.

" What the true meaning of a Fight for Fortune is,
Good fortune or ill-fortune—which most perilous?"

The Comedy of Dreams.

CHARLES COTTON, rising early, went into the village to see his Uncle Richard. That aged gentleman, drowsily living on his bread and cheese fortune, could not make out his erratic nephew, who seemed always to be meeting with fresh adventures. He received him with a certain amount of alarm. He was leaning over the garden gate amid a noble bloom of chrysanthemums when Charles arrived.

"So you are back safe, Charles," said the old boy, in a tremulous voice. "Nothing bad against you, as they said there was? Is it all right?"

"All right, uncle," he said, cheerily. "I never did anything dishonest, and don't mean to begin. The Squire knows I had nothing to do with that robbery, and the people who did it are found out. So here I am again, ready to live with you and do my old work."

"Old Wrangel has got a new hand on," said Richard Cotton, fretfully. "And Emily and Sarah and Jane all say you're too stuck up. And Jenkins declares he'll have you murdered—I don't know why. You won't do much good staying here."

"I mean to stay, for all that," said Charles Cotton, carelessly. "If you won't have me, uncle, I can find a place somewhere; and if Wrangel doesn't want me, I can find work for myself. I'm going to see him now."

"Blood's thicker than water," said the old man to himself, as Cotton strode off. "He's a fine lad, that, though he seems always doing something main queer. I'll stick to un right through."

Cotton went on to Wrangel's. Wrangel was in his workshop, a long low building full of materials for pumps and tanks, with sheets of uncut glass, and other necessities of his vocation. He was hard at work, with one or two assistants. When he saw Cotton, he said :

"Hallo, my boy! Back again! Come

in and drink a glass of home-brewed ale."

And he led him into his sanctum, where he made up the accounts, for which the county people often kept him waiting much longer than they ought.

"Well, Charles," said Wrangel, as they drank their ale, "I've filled up your place just now. I can't send the young man away—his name's Hyslop, and he teaches in the Sunday School, and he's very attentive to Sarah. You know how religious she is. If Hyslop would marry Sarah and get out of this, why I should be only too glad to have you back. For a young fellow you use the diamond better than anybody I have known."

"And I didn't steal Miss Englehurst's diamonds," said Cotton, laughing. "Well, Mr. Wrangel, if you should want help, I am willing : but I must work for my living, and I know that any good workman can get his living in England. And how are the young ladies ? May I see them ?"

"Sarah's gone to morning church, I think, but Emily and Jane are in the garden. They'll be glad to see you."

They were there. They were glad to see him. Scrofulous Jane and partridge-breasted Emily had given up all hope of entrapping him, but they forgave him, and could not well help liking him. And the three had a pleasant chat, wherein he was congratulated on not being exactly a thief.

Next, determined to assert himself in the village, he went on to Jenkins's, and called for a glass of ale. Jenkins was stouter than ever, and the unhappy female who falsely passed as his wife was thinner and more miserable. Cotton, on entering, found a good many of his sworn enemies in the bar, but the fire of adventure had animated his courage, and he cared not. So he talked to Jenkins concerning the weather and the crops, topics suitable to his stolid intellect, but the landlord gave only a surly snort, while the landlady looked on with a sulky sneer.

As Charles Cotton came away from the Five Horseshoes, he met Castelcicala, who was coming down the village at a rapid pace, with Harold at his heels. Have I mentioned Harold before, the Squire's favourite bloodhound, a grand young dog, all gentleness and power? Harold and the Marquis were great friends. Dogs have considerable choice in friendship. Harold, though loyal to his master as a dog ought

to be, had a personal affection for Castelcicala. He romped along gaily, the tawny
old boy, his short mane quivering with
pleasure.

"So you have been visiting your old
friends, Cotton," said the Marquis; "I
hope they are all right."

"Thanks, yes," he replied. "It is
pleasant to see old friends when you have
been unexpectedly taken away."

"You talk platitudes, my dear boy,
and you are right. Platitude and English weather go together, like ham and
bread-and-butter in a sandwich. How
English ladies come to be perfection in
English weather, I shall never comprehend."

"We are a strong race, I suppose," said
Cotton. "Don't you want your breakfast,
Marquis?"

"I do," he said, emphatically. "But as we walk up to the Hall, I want to tell you two things. The Squire and I have had a long talk about you. He is very angry with himself that through him you have been falsely accused. I have told him, what I know to be true, that you have more brains in your head than most young fellows in your position, which arises doubtless from your gentle blood. He wants you to accept from him, keeping it a profound secret, five hundred a year for ten years, using it as you will—either to push you on in your trade or to give you a noble English education. Do you accept?"

"My God!" said Charles Cotton; "there are few men as generous as the Squire! Tell me, Marquis, ought I accept?"

"That depends," replied Castelcicala, "on the use you would make of it. Five hundred a year is not much for a man with fifty thousand a year to give away. If your idea is to make yourself a man, in the highest sense of the word, I should say: Take it and try."

"But is it not like being a mere beggar; a pauper?"

"No; decidedly no. The Squire feels that he has done you ill by a suspicion of you. He remembers the great service you did his daughter. He also feels, through what I have told him, that he can in some degree repay by helping you on in the world. I say, accept. Were such an offer made to me in your position, I should not hesitate. I should believe the time might come when, in some way or other, I might repay my benefactor, many times over, perchance. Remember that there are greater gifts than those of money."

"I will accept," he said after a long pause. "I suppose it seems absurd for a person like me to talk of rejecting five hundred a year for ten years. But I am doubtful whether I ought to take it, and I am doubtful whether it will do me good. You see I can always earn thirty shillings a week, and this is almost ten pounds a week. And as to going to a university, am I fit for it? They would all laugh at me."

"Fitter than most," said the Marquis. "If they laugh at you punch their heads. That is English etiquette, I believe. But really, Cotton, I am glad you have accepted

the Squire's offer, for he means it in true
kindness, and it will give you a great
chance in life, which I believe you can use.
Don't think of yourself as under an obliga-
tion. Some day you may do as much for
the Squire as he now does for you."

" I wish I may," said Cotton.

" Now," said the Marquis—they were
loitering slowly up the avenue—" I have
one more thing to say to you. Keep what
I say secret. You are in love."

" Indeed no," he replied, blushing suddenly none the less.

" You are in love with Cecilia Englehurst, Mr. Cotton," said Castelcicala, in his
straightforward way, " and I am not surprised at it, nor, indeed, would anyone who
once has seen that beautiful girl. Perhaps,
when you have won your spurs, you may

also win her. I am your rival, to this
extent. She is quite the loveliest creature
I have ever seen ; and, if she showed a sign
of love, she would madden me with love, and
the man who stood in my way at that
instant would soon reach Hades. But she
shows no sign, and I would not for the
world trouble her maiden mind ; and, perchance, when you approach her, who love
her, I know, there may be a tremour of
delight. I am very frank, you see. I
should not regret your winning her. I
could not love any woman who did not love
me."

Cotton found it rather difficult to follow
the Marquis's impassioned talk. The
impetuous Italian was too much for him.
But he said—

"Miss Englehurst is too far above me

for me to think of loving her. May I not worship her at a distance? You, Marquis, are happier, and can meet her as an equal. I would never marry a woman unless I were her equal."

Castelcicala laughed.

"You are proud. I saw you had the English pride in you when I met you first. Do you remember? You were fishing in the Engle. You said you were not a gentleman, but a workman. I said a man might easily be both. I say more now : no man can be a gentleman unless he is also a workman. Work is chivalry. The man who elaborately does nothing, and enjoys his own selfish existence, ought to be suppressed. I would have him publicly flogged. Ninety-nine men out of the hundred have to work somehow, or they could not live. So the worst examples of selfish indolence are among the women. I saw a letter from a lady not long ago, who really had a quick brain, in which she catalogues her ailments, and then says : 'I seem better than I am.' I know her. There's nothing the matter with her. .She's married to a stupid fellow enough, and she wants other men's admiration, and is rather too old and dried up to get it. Flatter her ironically, and she seems better at once. Why can't she do some good in the world? She has plenty of money, and might make others better than they seem."

"You seem indignant, Marquis," said Cotton, laughing. "This unfortunate lady has made you angry."

"O, she's only a vain elderly fool; but I am so great an admirer of the English

ladies that I don't care to see them degene-
rate. Of course, she cannot be of your
best blood. The true patrician lady does
not brood selfishly over her own ailments.
Her father was a parson, I believe, and
she married some very rich tradesman—a
Unitarian, I rather think—and so she has
not the high courtesy and courage of the
true English lady—the most beautiful
creation of God."

"Are you not disloyal to the ladies of
Italy, Marquis ?" asked Cotton.

"No. They are very charming, but I
prefer the English—even as I prefer
Chaucer to Boccaccio, Shakespeare to
Dante, Byron to Ariosto. I have a strong
infusion of English blood in me. My father
married Claudia Branscombe, of Branscombe, in Devon. My grandfather married

Christina Cotton, daughter of a well-known Admiral Cotton. That fact was one reason why I first took interest in you, for I felt no doubt that we were of the same family. I quarter the arms of Cotton, the cotton hanks; and I therefore regard you as a cousin, and, as your sound English adage says, 'Blood is thicker than water.'"

Curious that two such different men as old Richard and the Marquis should have quoted the proverb that day as to Charles Cotton. It is a proverb on which a strong lay sermon might be preached. Blood *is* thicker than water; and if human beings were wise, family relationship would be a much stronger and healthier thing than it is. Now, that is one thing in which Italy does excel England. No rich Castelcicala would desire to be freed from the presence of a poor Castelcicala; and as to letting him starve, as some English families of great wealth do their relations, it would be a municipal disgrace to him.

While the Marquis talked, they were walking back to Englehurst Hall.

"We shall be in capital time for breakfast, Cotton," said Castelcicala. "Don't say a word to the Squire about this; he hates being thanked for anything. By-and-by we'll have a talk as to what you had better do with yourself. I have already formed an idea on the matter. You gradually form yours, and we will exchange our notions. But meet the Squire and Miss Englehurst just as usual."

So they breakfasted. The Squire and the Marquis and the Abbé talked on some abstruse scientific question which had just

turned up at a meeting of the Astroäl-
chymic Association; neither Charles Cotton nor Cecilia could follow them, so got
the conversation all to themselves. I believe the question started by the Abbé was
whether Gauss's method of inscribing in a
circle a regular polygon of two hundred
and sixty-seven sides was the most easy.
Why anybody should want to do anything
so dreadful was the question that struck
Cis Englehurst; and she was quite glad
of some one to talk to who could not be
expected to have any such frightful forms
of knowledge. And what a delight was it
to Charles Cotton to have his dainty-
flavoured tea poured out by the fairest
hand imaginable into cups of priceless
china! What a delight to help her to the
crisp rasher, the omelet, the aspic of ban-

tam's eggs. Cotton acquitted himself very well, all things considered. Ignorance of social rules is very sad, of course, and it would be quite right to cut a man who took his olives with a fork or his cheese with a knife. But on this occasion Cotton found no great difficulty; bacon hath no special etiquette, and the only rule about tea is that you must not cool it by pouring into a saucer. So, while Gauss's polygon was thrown to and fro by these clever talkers, each of whom had a different idea on the impracticable topic, Cis and Charles talked mere nothings.

"You don't care much about polygons, I suppose?" she said.

"I remember a geometrical gentleman," said Cotton, "who had drawn a polygon of many sides with much care. Perhaps it was the very one the Abbé is talking about. The figure vanished; probably the servant-maid lighted his study fire with it. He cried out indignantly, 'Where is my polygon?' 'Your Polly gone,' exclaimed his wife. 'Who is your Polly, I should like to know?' I fear it took him some time to explain."

Cis laughed musically.

"Mathematicians had better not marry, I think," she said. "The best of them, they say, are senior wranglers. I shouldn't care much for a senior person or a man who wrangles. Give me a junior flirter."

Cis, you see, talked gay nonsense. She was a girl of the true sort, her father's daughter, to whom an evil thought was a thing impossible. She was as full of innocent fun as a lark is of song. I have said that her favourite poet was Keats, but she had Mat Prior on her book-shelf, and could enjoy him ; and she had read Tom Jones intelligently. There was never a purer rivulet of soul running through a lady's brain.

The discussion concerning the polygon of 257 sides grew so brisk that the Squire and the Abbé and the Marquis went off together to the library, having eaten but little breakfast, in order to draw a diagram and test the question. Cis and Charlie were left alone : they exchanged an intelligent smile when they found themselves *tête-à-tête*.

"Those dreadful mathematics !" said Cis. "I once had a governess who tried to teach me Euclid, and I told her I thought she ought to have been Mrs. Euclid. She was exactly the shape of an isosceles triangle in that horrid fifth proposition. I told her so, and I verily believe she boxed my ears, the wretch!"

"Wretch, indeed!" said Charles Cotton. "Those pink shells ought not to have been injured, however naughty you were in your babyhood."

"It wasn't in my babyhood, Mr. Cotton," she said; "I was old enough to know better. I ought to have learnt my Euclid, and got as far as the sixth book at least. I didn't do it, and so I am a frivolous young woman, in a time when everybody is either scientific or theological."

"Which do you like best, science or theology?"

"Neither," she said. "I've got the good sound religion I learnt in my youth, and I can't conceive what a girl wants of

science, unless she has unusual cleverness
that way. I haven't. I give it all up
hopelessly. I can no more remember the
number of the planets than the names of
the Kings of England. I have put to
flight many governesses, in one way and
another. It's an odd thing to be an only
daughter, Mr. Cotton, and to have one
teacher after another, each with her own
crotchet. One is bilious and pious; another
believes implicitly in 'Mangnall's Questions'; another in 'Colenso's Arithmetic';
another in 'Whittaker's Pinnock's Goldsmith's History of England.' I have tried
all these, and ever so many more, and
seldom had one for longer than a month.
It became such a bore to papa that he
said,

"'I'll have no more governesses. Go

into the library and take down books and read. If you want anything explained, come to me.'"

"A perfect way to educate a lady. But I suppose there are lots of things you don't know, Miss Englehurst?"

"I should think so. I am delightfully ignorant." By this time they had wandered from the breakfast-room into a charming conservatory, full of warmth and fragrance and colour. "I don't know the names of a tenth of the plants here. Is it any good to know names? I love the flowers, and I sometimes almost think they love me; and, if I want to know their names, I can ask the gardener. Now, am I right, Mr. Cotton?"

"I think you are always right. And if I wanted to give you your scientific name,

Miss Englehurst, I should not ask the gardener. I should call you——"

" What ?" she said.

" Wisdom and Beauty. Is there such a
flower ?"

They wandered away through the vast
conservatories, and had a pleasant morning
to themselves. That polygon with 257
sides was a blessing unutterable—to Charles
Cotton at least. As to the dainty little
daughter of Englehurst, she did not quite
know her own mind. There would be
something romantic in marrying a glazier ;
especially so handsome and erudite a glazier as Cotton. But then the Marquis, a
knight of romance, with so superb a style,
with half a dozen palaces in Italy, with a
life to offer her of a sort entirely fresh and
rare. It is something to say for our come-

ly Charles Cotton that for a moment she could hesitate.

"It is time for luncheon, Mr. Cotton, I think," she said at length, looking at a Lilliputian bauble of a watch.

"Happiness must have an end," he said.

"Is luncheon the natural end to happiness? I hope you will not find it so to-day. We really have a very good cook."

As indeed it proved. Cotton stayed at Englehurst Hall another night, and it was rather lucky that he did. It seemed as if he were fated to have adventures. After the Squire had gone to bed, Castelcicala asked him to play billiards.

"I know nothing of the game," he replied.

"I'll soon teach you. Redi shall mark.

Come into the billiard-room and try."

So he learnt the game, and, having a keen eye and a firm wrist, soon played it as well as at all necessary.

"You will play capitally in time," said the Marquis. "Will he not, Redi?"

"Yes, excellency."

The valet was dismissed, for it grew late. They still stayed talking awhile. Castelcicala had a liking for this young Englishman, whose blood it seemed likely he shared. When they went up to their rooms, that in which Cotton had slept was found to be locked, probably by some blunder of the groom of the chambers.

"It is too late to make a fuss about his stupid mistake to-night," said the Marquis —indeed, it was four in the morning— "Come and turn in with me. I don't care for a male bedfellow; but this once it won't trouble us."

"I can sleep on the floor well enough," said Cotton.

"Not at all," said the Marquis. "You and I are friends now. There are some men I could not sleep with—whom, indeed, I shudder to touch. But when two people who are friends happen to be in a difficulty like this, why should they not make the best of it?"

So the Marquis and Cotton lay together. Cotton, however, could not sleep. The excitement of the day was too much for him. Cis Englehurst's coquetries had set his brain on fire. The Squire's generosity had filled him with excitement. What should he do? Could he make Cis love him? Would it be fair to her father?

Should he go to Oxford? Should he travel? There was a whirl in his brain which would have probably resulted in a series of nightmares but for a very unpleasant incident. Suddenly some sharp instrument was thrust into his chest, and he, being of unusual strength, caught with the grasp of a vice the wrist of the man who did the deed. The cry which he uttered awoke the Marquis.

END OF THE SECOND VOLUME.

LONDON: PRINTED BY MACDONALD AND TUGWELL, BLENHEIM HOUSE